Be Positive

The *Creating Success* series

Titles available are:

THE SUNDAY TIMES

Be Positive
A Guide for Managers

SECOND EDITION

Phil Clements

△ **KOGAN PAGE** | *CREATING SUCCESS*

For Heather

First published in 1995
Second edition 2000

Kogan Page Limited
120 Pentonville Road
London N1 9JN

© Phil Clements 1995, 2000

British Library Cataloguing in Publication Data

A CIP record for this book is available from the British Library.

ISBN 0 7494 3256 X

Typeset by Jean Cussons Typesetting, Diss, Norfolk
Printed and bound in Great Britain by Clays Ltd, St Ives plc

contents

introduction

- Show several people a glass of water which is neither full nor empty and you can be sure that some of them will say it's half full and some will say it's half empty.
- Go to a business meeting where someone has a bright, innovative idea and you can be sure that there will be some who want to talk about the benefits and others who will do all they can to prevent it happening.
- Ask people who provide a service what they think of the customer and you can be sure that some will have only bad, cynical things to say as if everything is too much trouble for them.

There is a common thread between people who metaphorically see the glass as half full, those who see challenges rather than problems and those who genuinely desire to provide a first-rate service to colleagues and customers. Positive attitude.

This book is about positive attitude as it relates to the skills of management. Think for a moment about all the skills you need to be a good manager. Communication, time management, motivation, planning, empowerment, leadership, decision making, negotiating ... the list goes on. For any of these management skills to be successful they need to be firmly grounded in a positive attitude.

There is a very real sense in which having a positive attitude is an essential requirement of successful management. Even getting the job in the first place will need a positive attitude. Selection techniques are becoming very effective at sifting out those who are not positive about themselves, their skills, their aims, the organisation and type of work they want to do. Taking just a small sample of statements from management recruiting adverts in the Sunday press reveals that potential employers are seeking people with attributes framed in terms such as:

- motivated;
- smartly presented;
- excellent communication skills;
- excellent interpersonal skills;
- high level of drive and determination;
- think effectively at strategic level;
- able to initiate and manage change;
- proven ability to lead;
- good negotiator;
- motivating team builder;
- dynamic with a real sense of urgency;
- strong presence;
- inspirational manager;
- capable of thinking laterally;
- creative in style;
- ability to create win/win/win deals.

And so the list goes on! Do you recognise yourself? Spot the attributes that will require a positive attitude and orientation in your management. Of course they all will. To put it quite bluntly, without a positive orientation you would have little hope of displaying any of these attributes; they all go hand in hand with quality management.

Short- or fixed-term contracts are an increasing feature of the management scene, and the job for life philosophy is receding. Can you really afford *not* to be positive in all you do? If nothing else, you no longer have *time* to be negative, even assuming you have the spare energy. Are you in an organisation where the responsibility and management levels are flattening out? Throughout the public and private sectors, managers, aspiring managers or even supervisors are suddenly finding themselves with greater managerial responsibility, more work, more decision making to do. Is this your experience? Then you need a positive attitude to cope.

'But I just wasn't born positive' I hear you cry. Never fear. You *can* learn to be more positive just as certainly as you can learn to communicate, manage your time or make decisions more effectively. We will be looking at what being positive really means, how it can be achieved and how it applies in a variety of settings. Throughout the book you will find short exercises, checklists and activities to help focus your learning, make you think and help you assess your progress. Be positive about doing them! You will get much more from this book if you do.

positive by nature or nurture?

After you have finished reading this chapter you should have a good idea about the following:

- What comprises a positive attitude?
- Are we born positive or is it something we can learn?
- What exactly *are* attitudes, where do they come from and how does this relate to being positive?
- How positive are you? Do you need to think about making any changes to become *more* positive?

what comprises a positive attitude?

This book is all about positive attitude, so it seems right that at the outset we gain a clear understanding of what those words mean. Sometimes a clue to what things *are* is to understand what they are *not*. In this case we are not saying that a person with a positive attitude is someone who goes around with a permanent grin or is always bubbly and laughing. Neither are we saying that a positive person never sees the negative side of things; indeed, as you read through the book you will find that a truly positive person not only recognises the negatives but also has the skills necessary to handle them.

So let's turn now to what being positive is. There are some key words and phrases that we might use to describe being positive:

- non-judgemental;
- in control of self and situations;
- being creative in thinking and planning;
- able to cope with and manage change;
- optimistic;
- able to communicate effectively all the attributes above.

For the purpose of this opening chapter we will look very briefly at each of these. As we do so, think to what extent they apply to you. Later in the chapter there will be an opportunity for you to take a more structured look at how positive you are.

non-judgemental

Positive people tend to exhibit a non-judgemental approach to both other people and situations. They will tend to see the good in others rather than the bad and will try to make the best of bad situations. In management terms, such an approach is invaluable. If nothing else, it helps when making effective appraisals, particularly at times when it seems impossible to say anything good about someone. Positive people spend less time talking about people and more time talking about how to solve problems and get things done.

in control of self and situations

People with a positive attitude tend to exhibit a self-assurance about themselves and their ability. This is not to say that they are 'control freaks' – those who have to be in a position to direct and have power over absolutely everything they come into contact with. No, positive people are able to give control to others precisely because they do not have hang-ups about their own power. Positive managers are therefore generally able to delegate effectively.

being creative in thinking and planning

You will probably be pleased to know that being creative doesn't just mean that you are good at painting or able to sit down and write music! In terms of management skills, being creative means the ability to *think* creatively, and this in turn means having the ability to generate fresh ideas, solutions and strategies to the problems and challenges which arise. Positive people can be relied upon to suggest a way forward; positive people tend to know where they are going.

able to cope with and manage change

The management of change is a subject which has exercised many writers on the theory of management. Positive people tend to be excited at the prospect of change because it is what they thrive on. It represents the opportunity to explore new areas, have new experiences and push back the barriers of what is possible. The reason that positive people are able to cope with change is that, being confident in themselves and their ability to adapt, cope and apply their skills to different circumstances, change does not represent a threat to them.

optimistic

Most people think of a positive attitude as being an optimistic one, and while this is true, as we go through we will see that it is much more than that. To be optimistic is to be cheerful, to 'look on the bright side' and generally to be hopeful for a better future. Of course, all these characteristics will be present to some degree or other in a person with a positive attitude, but some people are capable of a sort of blind optimism which doesn't take proper account of reality. This is far from being positive, which is firmly rooted in the real world and takes account of things as they are, not some vague idea of how they should be. Positive managers exhibit an optimism which is based on reality. To quote former prime minister Harold Wilson, 'I'm an optimist, but I'm an optimist who carries a raincoat.'

able to communicate effectively all the attributes above

This is the final ingredient of an effective, positive attitude. Our attitudes can only ever be known through the way we communicate them. To give an extreme example, if people never did anything, never spoke, never communicated non-verbally, it would be impossible to know what their attitudes were. In reality, we communicate all the time, either by what we do or what we say. Effective communication is a vital component of a positive attitude. We might have the best, most forward-looking and effective management plan the world has ever seen, but if we cannot communicate it ... forget it. Communication will never be far from our thinking about positive attitude.

are we born positive or is it something we can learn?

Ever since the concept of intelligence was floated, a debate has raged over whether a child is born with it, ie it is in the child's nature, or it can be developed given the right type of nurturing.

The argument has become known as the 'nature–nurture' debate. It doesn't only relate to intelligence; other aspects of the human experience have come under its umbrella. Are people born criminals? Are there *really* born leaders? If you are born shy, does that mean you have to stay that way for the rest of your life? The answers to these questions are not entirely straightforward and if you want to explore them fully you need to turn to the psychological theories of education and personality. Having said that, throughout this book we are going to make four assumptions which are central to its theme:

- ■ You are not born positive.
- ■ You can choose to be positive.
- ■ You can learn to be positive.
- ■ You can practise being positive or not as you choose.

These assumptions are important to all that follows because if you do not accept that being positive is something you can choose, then there is little hope for change. To paraphrase Charles Dickens in *A Christmas Carol*, if you don't believe that Marley was really dead, then no good can possibly come of the story.

If you still need convincing, try the exercise on page 9.

The way you think, your tastes, your politics are essentially learned and developed throughout your life. With the exception of your sense of humour and your drive and enthusiasm, which may be a bit of both, it would be surprising if your other ticks did not fall into the right hand column of boxes.

You may be thinking that all this is a bit extreme, but if you believe that you are born positive, or not as the case may be, then that is to accept that if you or those whom you manage are not positive, there is very little that can be done about it. This is not so. Undoubtedly, genetics do have a part to play; nearly all of us are able to run, but very few will ever be world champions. Most people can write, but very few will ever write a block-busting novel. We can nearly all hum a tune, but we will never be Pavarottis or Dame Kiri Te Kanawas. But, to use the same illustrations, with practice or training we could all run faster than we do, write better stories or sing more tunefully. So it is with adopting a positive attitude. You can be better at it. As a starting point it needs you to be positive about the possibilities for change!

Think about the following aspects of your life. For each one tick the box which most applies to you, ie

1. You definitely think you were born this way.
2. You are like this because of what you have been taught or the way you have been influenced.
3. You think it is a mixture of both.

	1 Born	2 Chosen	3 Mixture
The way you vote	☐	☐	☐
Your attitude towards money	☐	☐	☐
Your attitude towards race	☐	☐	☐
What you think about environmental matters	☐	☐	☐
Your sense of humour	☐	☐	☐
Your musical tastes	☐	☐	☐
Your drive and energy	☐	☐	☐
The newspaper you now read	☐	☐	☐

---

what exactly *are* attitudes?

There is one point which all attitudes have in common and that is that they are *towards* something and they represent our overall inclination (see Figure 1.1 below).

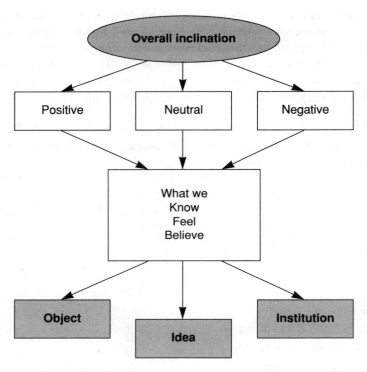

Figure 1.1 *Attitudes*

Defining a concept such as 'attitude' is notoriously difficult, and over the years psychologists have made many attempts. We shall see another example of the difficulty later when we think about personality. Having said that, most would agree that a definition of attitude should include certain key features. These are that attitudes will be:

■ consciously held beliefs or opinions;
■ positive or negative;
■ emotionally charged or at least contain an element of feeling;
■ a stimulus or disposition for action.

We have attitudes towards almost everything in life including, as you can see in Figure 1.1, objects (which include people), ideas and institutions. The point of this book is that where those attitudes concern management skills they need to be positive.

Think for a moment about the following statement:

> A positive attitude is probably the greatest gift a manager can have.
> Do you agree? ☐   Disagree? ☐

If you agree with the statement, the likelihood is that you will find yourself nodding in agreement frequently as you read through and do the exercises. If you disagree, then presumably you believe that there is a greater gift that a manager can have. If this is the case, please read through anyway, keep an open mind (which in itself is a sign of a positive attitude) and come back to this page when you have finished and ask yourself the question again.

Positive attitude in management is an attribute which enhances any or all of the management skills, but it cannot exist in a vacuum. For this reason there will be many examples of how a positive attitude links with these skills. In the exercise that follows you are invited to make a brief assessment of your own positive attitude.

Consider each of the key words or phrases which were introduced on page 5 of this chapter. In each case, calibrate your own scale by thinking about a time in your management experience when you were at either end of the two possible extremes relating to that characteristic.

Example: Think when you have been most judgmental as a manager and least judgmental. Let the most be 1 and the least 10. For each of the subsequent characteristics do the same. Then rate yourself on the scale according to how you see yourself at this moment. Are you at either extreme or are you somewhere in between?

Judgmental							Non-judgmental		
1	2	3	4	5	6	7	8	9	10

Not in control of self and situations							In control of self and situations		
1	2	3	4	5	6	7	8	9	10

Not creative in thinking and planning							Creative in thinking and planning		
1	2	3	4	5	6	7	8	9	10

Unable to cope with and manage change							Able to cope with and manage change		
1	2	3	4	5	6	7	8	9	10

Pessimistic								Optimistic	
1	2	3	4	5	6	7	8	9	10

Unable to communicate effectively							Able to communicate effectively		
1	2	3	4	5	6	7	8	9	10

There is, of course, no definitive score of positive attitude. To a certain extent you have to decide how positive you are at the moment and whether things need to change for you. You can probably also think of other characteristics which you believe are indicative of a positive attitude and they may be just as valid. Having said all that, the higher your score in the above exercise, the more likely you are to have a positive attitude in your management.

a positive management orientation

Before bringing this chapter to a close it is worth identifying another way of seeing being positive in management. Later in the book we will think about the way people hold different ways of seeing the world. If you glance back at the introduction you will see a list of attributes of managers that are required by prospective employers. Now of course it would be unreasonable or unrealistic for all of those things to be required of any one individual. We all have strengths and weaknesses. But if we were to take a helicopter view of a person who was characterised by a majority of those attributes we might be tempted to describe it as rather stronger than just a positive attitude. In many ways a collection of attributes such as those listed represents a positive way of seeing the world, or at least the world of management. The attributes are a positive orientation towards management. So in the chapters that follow, 'positive attitude' will be used to describe a person's positive approach in relation to specific attributes, whereas 'orientation' will be used to mean a positive approach to the collection of management attributes we will be thinking about.

summary

In this chapter we opened the discussion by trying to capture the essence of a positive attitude.

■ It is not a permanent grin.
■ It is represented by a set of characteristics which range from being non-judgmental to being able to communicate effectively.
■ Being positive is something which can be learned, and which can be developed and practised.

■ Attitudes are overall inclinations towards something.
■ You were challenged to assess your own level of positive attitude.
■ The chapter concluded with a brief explanation of the notion of 'positive orientation'.

the science of being positive

Adopting a positive attitude of the type we identified in Chapter 1 is not just a fashion which happens to be flavour of the month. In this chapter we identify and explore the ways in which the origins, benefits and effects of a positive attitude have their roots in psychology, sociology and educational theory. By the time you have read this chapter I hope you will have been stimulated to think about:

- personality, and the links between positive attitude an optimism.
- human behaviour in groups, including positive and negative reinforcement and encouragement, and how behaviour breeds behaviour.
- how being positive affects learning; do we really learn from our (negative) mistakes?
- how what we have learned so far relates to a case study of a manager with a very negative orientation to management.

where does personality fit into being positive?

Some ideas from psychology:

Start by having a go at saying what personality *is*. Write a definition in the box below.

How did you get on? My guess is that unless you are a trained psychologist, it was harder than you might have expected. With such a commonplace idea as personality we all think we know what it means until challenged to define it. It might surprise you to know that even as long as 40 years ago one psychologist listed as many as 50 attempts to define personality. Having said that, in more recent times some common features of definitions have emerged. These are that:

■ Personality is stable in the sense that we do not readily turn into fundamentally different people.
■ Personality is organised, meaning that the components of our personalities are related to and have an effect on each other.
■ Personality results from an interaction between our innate biological mechanisms and the environment.
■ Personalities are distinct. Put simply, people are special.

Take a moment to review the features that a definition of personality should contain and see if your own definition contains them. Do you need to revise yours in any way or will it do?

So what has all this got to do with positive attitude in management? Well, having seen what should be in the definition of personality, these factors can now be applied to what we normally refer to as personality, namely:

- affective traits; simply things to do with emotions, emotionality, feelings and moods;
- sentiments; the stance taken or sets of feelings towards people or situations;
- attitudes;
- interests;
- ideals.

So now you can see that there is in fact a very strong link between the psychology of personality and positive attitude in management. Attitudes are an essential ingredient of our personalities. A positive attitude will also be a component of our sentiments, and will be related to our moods, feelings and emotions.

How our personalities develop is a question which continues to vex psychologists, but as with other aspects of our development, for example intelligence, there is a balance between nature and nurture, or heredity and environment.

Thinking about the balance between heredity and environment in the development of personality, mark on the line where you think the balance should lie.

Heredity_____**Environment**

While heredity does play an important role, most would agree that the environment is crucial to the development of personality, particularly in young children and as they move through the various stages of development into adulthood.

optimism

Many people use the ideas of optimism and pessimism to describe another's personality. In fact, it has such a strong labelling effect that we might say he or she *is* an optimist or a pessimist. This has implications for our thinking about positive attitude, for while we might describe a person as an optimist or pessimist, we rarely actually mean that they are always one or the other. We cannot use the words to describe all there is to know about a person's personality.

Think about two periods in your life: one where you felt really optimistic and one where you felt really pessimistic. Make a note in the appropriate boxes below of how you were feeling.

A pessimistic time	**An optimistic time**
What was going on at the time? What was making you feel the way you did?	What was going on at the time? What was making you feel the way you did?

If you are able to identify two examples from your own experience, there must be times when you are one thing or the other. You are not condemned to be either an optimist or a pessimist for your whole life. In developing your positive attitude in management, try to hook on to the factors which you identified as making you optimistic.

So, your personality and your positive attitude are interlinked. Let's draw the threads of this section together in summary form:

- Attitudes are a component of personality and they can develop and change.
- It is not enough to say that we are born this way or that way and nothing about our personalities can ever change.
- While personality taken as a whole is relatively stable in most people, its components can and do vary. This is what makes us humans not robots.
- We have a great deal of control over the manifestation of our personality, namely our behaviour, and it is to this topic that we turn in the next section.
- Optimism and positive attitude are closely linked.

positive attitude in work situations

Some ideas from psychology and sociology:

Psychologists and sociologists have been studying attitudes in the workplace for many years. In this section we shall take a brief look at some of the ideas to emerge, concentrating as always on the positive aspects of such attitudes. We can group these ideas best into four sections.

1. attitudes and actions

We can summarise some of the thinking about attitudes and actions as follows:

- *Attitudes and actions are connected, although not always in the way that we expect.* The equation goes both ways in the sense that attitudes can affect actions but actions may also have an effect on attitudes. For example, a person whose attitude towards time-keeping was very negative in that he or she did not feel it at all important would, in all likelihood, show this by a lack of punctuality. On the other hand, a person who previously had a positive attitude towards time-keeping but, for whatever reason, was late on a couple of occasions and found that it was either not noticed, went unchallenged or in some other way did not have too many negative consequences, might have his or her attitude towards punctuality eroded towards the negative.

■ *Strength of attitude is a measure of its importance to someone.* People who feel strongly for or against something are more likely to behave in ways which reinforce their positive or negative attitude. This is well illustrated by the way prejudice operates. The more strongly a person feels about, say, minority groups, the more likely it is that their positive or negative feeling will have a direct effect on the way they act.

■ *Attitudes and actions are linked to personal freedom of choice.* This may need a little more explanation. People who work in a non-managerial direct production or service type job will often have little choice over what they do, when they do it and so on. This greatly reduces personal freedom of choice and may well have a strong influence on attitudes and actions. On the other hand, managers, professionals and others will often have far greater freedom of personal choice and be more in control of their own destiny; this leads to a more fertile ground for the growth of positive attitude.

2. what factors impact on occupational attitudes?

In the section above we identified the fact that attitudes and actions are linked. Now try the next exercise.

In the list below are several factors which have been identified by psychologists as having an impact on attitudes in the workplace.

Think about each in turn, then rank them in order of importance according to your experience. Give the most important 1 and the least important 5.

☐ Wage levels

☐ Working conditions

☐ Management behaviour

☐ Variety of type of work

☐ Freedom of choice of the worker

It's not hard to see how some of the factors can affect attitudes. Low pay, boredom with repetitive work, feeling of lack of control and poor working arrangements will inevitably have a strong influence and may well tend to pull the person involved towards negative attitudes. But the crucial question is how highly did you rate management behaviour as a strong determinant of attitudes?

As a manager you:

■ may not be able to influence wage levels directly;
■ may not be able to do much about the working conditions;
■ may not be able to make the nature of the work more intrinsically interesting.

But what you *will* be able to do is influence the attitudes of those who work for you by your own behaviour and, as we noted above about the link between attitudes and behaviour, your attitudes will influence your behaviour, and your behaviour will influence your attitudes. What indicators are there of the state of attitudes in your place of work?

3. measures of work behaviour – attitude indicators

There are many measures of work behaviour which will be useful as indicators of the presence of positive attitudes in both you and those whom you manage. In the next exercise you are invited to consider a range of indicators of attitude in the workplace. Think of them as a litmus test.

There is no expectation that you will blindly accept these as necessarily being relevant to your own situation; they may not be. For this reason, you are in each case invited to consider each attitude indicator carefully. Make a note of its strengths and weaknesses as an indicator, and then decide whether you feel this will be useful to you as an indicator of attitude in your own work situation. Mark this by putting a tick in the 'relevant to me' column or leave it blank if the indicator is not useful in your situation.

4. ideas about motivation

There is a strong link between positive attitude in management and motivation, and this chapter would not be complete if we did not briefly consider some ideas about motivation which have developed in psychology. There are three main aspects to motivation which can be inferred from what we observe.

Attitude indicator	Strengths of the indicator	Weaknesses of the indicator	Relevant to me
Work performance – output			
Work performance – service to customers			
Work performance – attention to detail			
Work performance – task and objective oriented			
Punctuality			
Absenteeism			
Relations with colleagues			
Relations with management			
Relations with customers			
Labour turnover			
Supports organisational aims			
Active, alternative job seeking			
Your own indicator:			✓
Your own indicator:			✓

need

Need has a strong relationship with motivation. At a biological level, hunger or thirst will create a need to eat or drink. At a higher level, people may have needs generated in the mind. For example, people who live very active and full lives may have a need to continue doing so even after they retire. These needs tend to motivate the individual to take action or behave in a way which will satisfy the need.

drive

Drive is closely related to need in that it refers to the strength of energy the person invests in fulfilling a need. Take as an example a career person who feels a strong need for power or success. The drive he or she demonstrates may be quite outside the experience of most ordinary people whose need for power or success is less sharply focused.

incentive

Incentive refers to the motivating power of an objective or goal. Objectives or goals which people are motivated to attain are generally called positive incentives. Objectives or goals which people try to avoid are called negative incentives. Looking again at our career/success oriented individual, the incentive will quite often be 'to get to the top', and this will be one of the most powerful incentives in that person's life.

There are many life incentives which drive people; one thing we can say is that we are generally driven by a complex combination of them, and that we are all different in this respect. Some examples include:

■ the acquisition of money or material wealth;
■ spiritual enlightenment;
■ knowledge;
■ power;
■ pleasure/happiness;

■ success;
■ fitness;
■ fame.

Understanding what drives us will help us to understand and inform the attitudes we adopt. It is important that you as a manager have a good understanding of your own motivation, through understanding your own needs, drives and incentives. It will help you to understand why you are more or less positive towards some things than others.

You may like to try the next set of questions, but as the answers will be quite personal, it might be a good idea to write them on a separate sheet of paper so that you can throw it away afterwards.

Thinking about your situation at work:

What personal needs do you find repeatedly occurring?

What drive(s) do you experience and on what are they focused?

What longer-term incentives do you feel you are addressing in your work life?

Taking all the answers to the three questions above together, do you think your motivation tends to make you more positive in your attitudes or less positive?

☐　More positive
☐　Less positive

If you think your motivation makes you less positive in your attitudes, what changes could you make to redress the balance?

---

do we really learn from our mistakes or is learning a more positive affair?

Some ideas from educational theory:

We need to establish an idea which has still some way to go to being accepted by many managers. Managers have a responsibility for training and educating those they manage. Look at some of the ways in which this is true.

Managers are responsible for:

■ the development of their staff;
■ appraising their staff;
■ the welfare, contentment and satisfaction of their staff.

The sad fact is that many managers still do not accept that these responsibilities have anything to do with training. They see training as being the responsibility of the personnel officer or the training officer, but not themselves. In true learning organisations the responsibility for training will be equitably shared between the organisation, the line management and the individual. The problem is that when managers do not see themselves as having anything to do with training, their attitude towards it is usually far from positive. In some circumstances it might actually be obstructive, by denying a member of staff a learning opportunity.

Since training and personnel development are so directly linked with managing staff, let's look at some of the ways in which being positive can be brought to bear on training.

we do not necessarily learn from our mistakes

Not long ago I was working in my loft doing some plumbing work. One of the roof beams protrudes out into the loft space; it is hard, obvious and I hit my head on it, not once, not twice, but three times over a period of two days! I had three small scars to prove that I certainly did not learn from my first mistake.

Mistakes are essentially negative and we tend not to learn best from negative experiences but positive ones. Learning from mistakes can happen but generally only with the essential ingredient of feedback or reflection. So if I had really stopped to think about why I was hitting my head on the beam in my loft, I might have worked out that I needed to pad it in some way, or mark out a different route to avoid the same situation.

People are often not capable of turning their mistakes into positive learning experiences for a number of reasons:

- They may not know what they have done wrong.
- They may know that they have done wrong but not understand why it happened.
- They may know that they have gone wrong somewhere, may even understand why it happened, but have no idea about how to put it right in the future.

■ Their self-image may be so dented by the negative experience of failure that they will need the support of a manager to pick themselves up and make the best of the situation.

The point is that in each case a positive attitude towards learning or training is needed to get the best from the situation. This is the responsibility of you, the manager.

Let's look at some ways in which positive attitude and learning are linked, drawing on ideas from education and training.

be positive about the learning and development of your staff

Thinking back to what we were saying about incentives and motivation, many people have little incentive to learn or self-develop because their expectations of themselves are so low. This is symptomatic of a negative attitude which you can remedy. Helping people to believe in themselves and therefore develop a positive attitude will do wonders for their expectations. There are many ways in which this can be done, but before we note some of them, let's start by laying out a couple of assumptions on which the next section is based:

■ You have accepted, maybe in partnership with the individual and with a personnel or training officer, some responsibility for training the staff who work for you or whom you supervise.
■ You have accepted some responsibility for supporting their personal development, by planning, making resources or training opportunities available and giving them the encouragement necessary.

Here are some actions you can take to achieve a good, positive attitude in training, learning and development.

never put the person down

Probably the single biggest barrier to adults learning is a fear of looking stupid, asking what is perceived to be a silly question or in some other way being put down by either colleagues, fellow learners, teachers, trainers or managers.

be positive about raising expectations

But do it realistically! Another huge barrier to learning and development in adults is the level of their own expectations. In terms of numeracy, many people seem to accept without question the validity of statements such as:

- ■ 'I was never any good at maths' (and therefore couldn't possibly be so now).
- ■ 'I'm no good with computers' (and therefore will avoid them at all costs).
- ■ 'I'm better at a job where I don't have to meet people' (what I really need is some help with being assertive).
- ■ 'I'm just not up to that promotion' (others are far better than me).
- ■ 'I can't spell' (no one has ever tried to help me spell better or I have never heard of spellcheckers on word processors).
- ■ 'I don't know enough to do better than I am doing at the moment' (I have never even considered a training course or further qualification).

By now you will almost certainly have seen that such thinking is negative and will not help the person to develop. Yet, with a little positive attitude in terms of interest, encouragement, needs analysis, and support in helping you find out what learning opportunities are available, you can turn low expectations into high expectations. This, in turn, will affect the attitudes of the person concerned because now he or she will be motivated by a positive rather than negative incentive, ie something that person wants to achieve rather than avoid.

give reward

Let's face it, we do not generally live in a climate that looks for the good rather than the bad. There is a tendency always to look for the negative and ignore the positive. So it is with giving feedback to learners and staff we are responsible for developing. In the next chapter we shall look in some depth at the art of giving good, positive feedback, but for the time being we will establish the point that if adults are to learn and reach their potential, they will need lots of positive encouragement and reinforcement of what they are doing well.

We need to overcome the obstacle that it is somehow *easier* to spot the negative points about a person's performance than the positive. A management skill that needs to be developed, particularly in relation to people-handling skills, is the art of looking for the good, finding it, describing it, and then feeding it back to the persons concerned in a way that will uplift and support but not patronise them. Never assume that an adult does not need a 'well done' occasionally! It is a good discipline to tackle any difficult person or situation about which you feel negative by making sure you start off by saying something good about the person or situation. It helps break the habit of always looking for the negative and rarely giving reward.

provide resources – develop a learning environment

If you are taking your responsibility for developing people seriously, you will need to provide the resources they require to take part in the process. Just knowing the direction in which to point them will work wonders. Here are some ideas about providing resources:

■ Give the person time to learn new skills.
■ Offer alternative training solutions such as distance learning, open learning, multimedia training, videos, self-instructional books.
■ Know and communicate the training policy (if there is one) of your organisation, and do what you can to forward it.
■ Create structures where mutual support becomes second nature.
■ Create a learning climate by encouraging reflection, analysis and action to achieve better results next time.
■ Keep asking, 'What can we learn from this?'

---

case study 2.1
the finance manager who failed to manage

Julian is a finance manager for a company in the service sector. The company arranges tours to England for people in the Far East. He has responsibility for financial planning, managing the procurement and allocation of resources, and since his role involves a budget of several million pounds this automatically gives him a place in the 'senior management team'. He has a small team of administrative staff who undertake a whole range of administrative functions including pay, overtime, purchasing, expenses and so on. It is noticeable that Julian's team members are often not happy. He has a bad relationship with the manager who has day-to-day responsibility for the administration group, and the group itself does not enjoy a good reputation in the company. The staff members are often on the receiving end of complaints about their unhelpful attitude, and although they appear always to be working to capacity, they never seem to be 'on top' of the work. The administration manager knows the last time she tried to confront Julian about the problems she and the administration group were experiencing, he held a grudge against her for several months.

At times of busy activity, Julian is known to take time off owing to him, but he will not allow others in the office to take time off then. When people, particularly the administration manager, take their problems to Julian, his response is usually to focus on his own issues and show no real sign of listening to the concerns of his staff. Whenever he is off and the administration manager tries to deputise for him, she finds that a great deal of information is not recorded but is stored in Julian's head. This often means that little can be done until he returns to work.

Julian's attitude and orientation towards his management is far from positive. In many ways he represents a stereotype of a particularly negative approach.

Write a brief summary of the areas in which you think Julian needs to develop a positive orientation towards his management. Use the information in this chapter as a basis for your analysis. You may also like to skip forward and briefly survey the 'five golden rules' for a positive attitude suggested in Chapter 7 and use these as a framework for your response.

You will no doubt have concluded that as a manager Julian has a way to go before he could be considered to have a positive attitude and orientation. You have probably identified a number of areas in which he needs to develop to be a positive manager. Assess the extent to which they match the ideas that follow.

Julian seems to be regularly breaking at least four of the five golden rules for being positive in his management. His approach to allowing himself time off when he denies it to others, however he might justify it, will be seen to be unfair by those for whom he is responsible. He is hardly being visionary in his approach to storing important information in his head. There may, of course, be a sense in which he is doing this with a very negative and manipulative motivation, namely that in his eyes it secures his position and enables him to exercise power over the company and effectively prevents anyone from taking his place. If this were true it would be important for the other members of the senior management team, or the board of directors, senior partners or whoever, to deal with this as a matter of urgency. No company should allow itself to be placed in a position where it could effectively be blackmailed by an employee who holds key information that is unrecorded anywhere.

Julian is not team oriented, he is negatively self-oriented. When a member of his team comes to him to discuss a problem the last thing he should do is talk about his own issues and focus on his own needs. This leads on to the fourth area of concern, namely that Julian is not being professional. Allowing himself to be seen to be unfair, failing to engage in the problem of the efficiency and happiness of the team for which he is responsible, and holding grudges when problems are identified are all traits of a manager who lacks professionalism.

The following points summarise some of the lessons about a positive orientation to management that are revealed in Julian's case study. You might like to consider whether you think there are more.

- Positive managers, when it comes to grudges, should develop bad memories.
- Positive managers do not feel threatened and have to resort to manipulative strategies to secure their position.
- Positive managers develop systems to ensure that outputs can be maximised with minimum inputs.

■ Positive managers are concerned about the welfare and happiness of all the staff who work for them regardless of personal preference for individuals.

■ Positive managers lead by example.

summary

In this chapter we have made the point that positive attitude is not just a trendy management trick but an essential ingredient of a variety of management skills. It is an approach to almost everything you do as a manager. You have had a look at a case study that illustrates a number of lessons that we can learn about being positive as managers. We have also noted that:

■ Personality arises as a result of both heredity and environment but the influence of environment or nurture should not be underestimated.

■ Attitudes and actions are linked.

■ Your behaviour will influence the occupational attitudes of others.

■ There are many potential attitude indicators you can use.

■ You were invited to think about your own needs, drives and incentives. Are any of these getting in the way of your positive attitude?

■ If mistakes are to be turned into positive learning experiences, they need feedback.

■ Be positive about the learning needs of your staff.

Learn to say something good!

the art of being positive

In the previous chapter we looked at some of the more theoretical aspects of adopting a positive attitude in your management and found that much of what we are saying has its roots in psychology, sociology and education. In this chapter we shall take a more practical view and think about positive attitude from the point of view of the practice of being positive. Specifically, by the time you have worked through this chapter, I hope you will:

- be able to sort out your definition of success and failure;
- have an understanding of what feedback is;
- recognise the importance of being able to receive positive feedback;
- be in a position to practise giving positive feedback;
- have considered the importance of being genuine;
- recognise the importance of developing a positive self-image;
- discover that being positive is not the same as not being negative.

Throughout this chapter we will touch on aspects of management, which are all dealt with in depth in other books in the series, but all of which benefit from being exercised with a positive attitude. Take a close look at Figure 3.1 which sets out some of the aspects of management skill which are improved by a positive attitude. There are a couple of blank lines for you to fill in any skills which you think are missing.

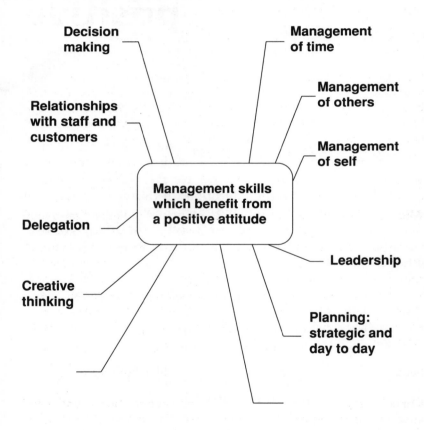

Figure 3.1 *Aspects of management skill improved by a positive attitude*

success and failure

How do you define success and failure? It's surprising how many people define them differently and yet a balanced, sensible view of success and failure is an important component of a positive attitude. See what you think about the following situations. Would you rate them successes or failures, or do you think it's not that simple to make a judgement?

Having left school at 16, **Brian** has, in the past, had few opportunities for educational development, but over the last four years has been studying for a degree in his spare time. He has worked very hard and was really hoping for at least an upper second class honours. Having taken his finals he is awarded an unclassified degree. Is Brian a success or a failure?

Success ☐   Failure ☐   Not that simple ☐

Alice has been doing the same job for several years and feels that she needs a change. Her company has internally advertised two vacancies which would be promotion for Alice. Job one represents a considerable step up for Alice, and would give her a managerial salary; job two would mean only a slight advancement for her and would keep her in a supervisory but not management grade. She is allowed to apply for them both, and really wants job one as she feels she is well qualified for it. She is offered job two. Is Alice a success or a failure?

Success ☐   Failure ☐   Not that simple ☐

Chris is very career minded. He feels the need for power and influence and is strongly driven towards that aim. His whole energy is directed towards his career, and having received one promotion, he then devotes himself to achieving the next. He doesn't much care for the people who get in his way and has little time to devote to the development of others around him because he is so inwardly focused. He frequently lands good business for the company, and eventually gets to the top. Is Chris a success or a failure?

Success ☐   Failure ☐   Not that simple ☐

Deborah works in a so-called 'caring' profession, working with the elderly. She has no ambition to be promoted even though every annual appraisal she has ever had has suggested that she has all the qualities needed to move into a managerial grade. She could easily earn a lot more money than she does, but finds that she is far less interested in the size of her pay packet than the people she works with for whom she genuinely cares. Deborah has few material possessions because her pay is so low. Would you rate Deborah a success or a failure?

Success ☐   Failure ☐   Not that simple ☐

It is quite likely that you have answered 'not that simple' to all of them. The fact is that success and failure are not always what they seem, and what is certain is that people define them in different ways.

The important thing is that the way *you* define success and failure will not necessarily be the way others define them. So, as a manager, it is important that you accommodate other views of success and failure as well. What does this mean in the examples above?

■ **Brian** got a degree, and although it may have not been what he wanted, to graduate after a poor start educationally can hardly be defined as a simple failure. If you were Brian's manager, it would be entirely right to stress the positive aspects of what he had achieved.

■ **Alice** did not achieve all that she had hoped for but she did achieve something. Were her expectations realistic in the first place? A positive outcome was that she has taken some first steps; with development and positive reinforcement, would she get the other job next time?

■ **Chris** has all the outward indications of success yet, of the three examples, and accepting that we know little about him, he might be the one who is actually the biggest failure in terms of his contribution as a manager of people.

■ Finally, **Deborah,** in many people's definition, would be classed as a failure and yet in terms of satisfying her own motivation and drive, she really succeeded and found fulfilment.

develop the art of being able to receive positive feedback

Let's start this section with an exercise.

Think of a situation in which you have done something well. A member of your staff who works directly for you approaches you and tells you how well they think you have done and how much they appreciate it. How might you react? Here are some possible responses. Tick those that reflect the way you are thinking.

1. I feel irritated that a junior member of my team should presume to give me praise. ☐
2. It's good to be appreciated. ☐
3. I'm paid to get results and do a job. I don't need praise. ☐
4. I'm slightly embarrassed.
5. I feel patronised. ☐
6. I must do work like this more often. ☐
7. I wonder what they want ... no one gives praise without a reason. ☐

8. I always thought they were a creep. ☐
9. I need to work out what went well so that I can
   repeat it. ☐
10. Thanks for that ... no qualification, just thanks. ☐

If you ticked, 1, 3, 4, 5, 7 or 8, the chances are that you need to do some work on receiving positive feedback. Many of us have become so used to operating in a world which just focuses on the negative that it has become difficult to accept positive feedback. If you find it difficult, do you think it will be any different for your staff? Bear in mind that if you find it difficult to *accept* positive feedback from others, this will almost certainly get in the way of your being able to *give* positive feedback. This leads us on to the next two sections of this chapter: some practical advice about giving positive feedback and some thoughts about being genuine.

give positive feedback

There is an old saying that 'practice makes perfect', and while this may be partly true, 'practice with feedback makes perfect' is probably truer. This goes back to what we were saying about how learning from mistakes, understanding why the mistake was made, reflecting on it and working out a way of doing better next time all make the learning far more effective.

'Feedback' is a term that has derived from technology, where, in a system, part of the output is fed back into the system which then helps it to make adjustments. A good example of feedback in a system is that of a car's heating and cooling system. A key output of the engine is energy in the form of heat. This output is nearly always measured by a thermostat, and when a given temperature is reached this is fed back in to the system and the cooling system increases its efficiency.

Without such feedback the engine would just continue to get hotter (or too cool) and eventually fail to do what it was supposed to.

The observable output of human beings is behaviour. We all rely to a degree on feedback to help us adjust that behaviour to suit the given circumstances. This giving and receiving of feedback can be verbal and non-verbal, and is a vital function in interpersonal relations. It is not the purpose of this book to go into all the issues that surround this, but as managers an understanding of the importance and processes of feedback is a vital component of a positive orientation.

A key difference between the thermostat feedback example above and the way humans handle feedback is that we all tend to have different views of the world, and in order to make sense of the world we make interpretations. Now presumably if most car thermostats had a brain, they would view heat in more or less the same way. The human feedback process is somewhat different in that positive feedback may be interpreted negatively and vice versa, and feedback may be ignored altogether.

Later in this section we will consider some guidelines for avoiding misinterpretation of feedback and even having it ignored, but for the time being we will consider what positive feedback in management terms is all about:

- establishing what went well about a particular behaviour and giving the appropriate reward;
- establishing what did not go well and helping the person to find out why;
- focusing on the behaviour not the person;
- being honest without being destructive;
- being specific and not making negative generalisations.

Before we move on to thinking about these in a little more detail, let's consider some short pieces of feedback and identify what is going wrong. Since we are learning about giving feedback, we will allow ourselves the licence of identifying the bad things; in real life, there will invariably be something positive to focus on!

Taking account of what positive feedback is all about as described in the bulleted list above, look at each of these in turn and decide what is, or could be, going wrong:

	Feedback	What is going wrong
1.	'Whenever I hear you speaking to a customer on the telephone I get irritated by your attitude.'	
2.	'To be perfectly frank, you will never make a good impression because you always look like a sack of potatoes.'	
3.	'You didn't meet the deadline, did you? Let's face it, you are just unreliable.'	
4.	'Well, you did as you were asked, but that's no more than would be expected. What I want to focus on is the things you could improve.'	
5.	'Well, you managed to upset the customer yet again. I have no idea why this happens every time.'	

In each case you should have spotted that the feedback was far from being positive. More specifically though (remember that being specific is a feature of positive feedback), you might have noted the following:

1. This feedback is making generalisations and is not specific. It is therefore negative feedback. The implication is that the person always does this ... is this really true? In any case, what attitude is being referred to? As feedback, such statements are almost useless.

2. This feedback purports to be honest. We often use 'let me be frank' as an opening gambit for saying something destructive. In this case, it probably is necessary to be honest. If the person's appearance is not up to scratch, particularly if they wear a uniform or corporate clothing of some kind, it may be necessary to be honest with them. But do not do it in a way which will seem to be an attack on them as a person. One tip here is to avoid giving this type of feedback when you are angry. In fact, any type of feedback given in anger is unlikely to come out as you intend. It will usually descend into an attack on the person, and the original offending behaviour will be forgotten!

3. In this one the person is the focus of the feedback where it should be the behaviour. 'You are unreliable' is labelling the person, and the positive way of dealing with this would be to try to identify why the deadline was not met and any specific occasions when it has happened before. Very often a person's failure to meet a deadline will not be entirely their own fault. Is there something you could have done to assist? Have you delegated too much responsibility? Is there any sense in which it is your fault?

4. It sounds as if the person giving this feedback is quite unused to giving praise. He or she is grudgingly acknowledging the fact that the person has done what was expected but, instead of letting that person take some pleasure in the feedback, is immediately moving on to negative things.

5. Finally, there is no attempt in this feedback to try to understand what went wrong. It is probably obvious

to all concerned that the customer is upset, but positive feedback would seek to find out why, without apportioning blame, and with the intention of making sure it did not happen again.

checklist for giving feedback with a positive orientation

The following checklist may help you focus on the key issues we have mentioned so far together with a few extras. If you develop the art of giving positive feedback, you will be well on the way to a positive orientation in your management. The checklist is presented in a form that will enable self-reflection on your part. How often do you achieve 'always'?

With regard to feedback I ...	Always	Sometimes	Never
Focus the feedback on the behaviour of the person, not their personality			
Allow the person to whom I am giving feedback to choose their response rather than dictate it to them			
Describe and give evidence of specific behaviours rather than general behaviours			
Introduce things I know rather than things I am guessing about or making inferences about			
Seek agreement with the person about my observations			
Avoid making value judgements about the person's behaviour			

With regard to feedback I ...	Always	Sometimes	Never
Harness the views and experiences of other people who are also in a position to observe the individual's behaviour			
Show ownership of the feedback by being honest and making 'I' statements, not pretending I am doing this on behalf of someone else			
Direct my feedback towards things that the receiver can take action on – not negotiate impossible goals			
Don't use feedback as a way of venting my own frustration or anger			
Keep it within manageable proportions for the receiver and don't try to overload them			
Check that the message I am giving is the same as the one they are receiving			
Make every effort to preserve and affirm the self-esteem of the receiver			

be genuine

Applying the skills of management with a positive attitude will inevitably mean there will be a need for you to be genuine. Insincerity and cynicism have no place in the development of a positive attitude towards your management.

People we deal with are usually far more perceptive than we give them credit for. Think of the times when you have known that someone was not being genuine in their attitude to *you*; what gave them away?

- ■ The words they used?
- ■ The tone of voice they adopted?
- ■ The content of what they were saying?
- ■ The non-verbal behaviour they used?
- ■ The lack of eye contact?

Take a moment to examine how genuine you are in the way you deal with those you manage.

Think through your personal answers to the following questions, if you wish making notes about examples of the circumstances giving rise to your answer.

Do I ever manipulate people to get my own way?

Is my concern for the success of the team based on a belief in the team or the credit I will get for it?

When a member of the team does well, do I really wish it was me?

Do I ever give praise grudgingly?

Do I really believe in the values and purpose of my organisation or do I just pay lip service to them?

```
┌──────────────────────────────────────────────────┐
│                                                  │
│                                                  │
│                                                  │
└──────────────────────────────────────────────────┘
```

Is there anything more important than getting the job done?

```
┌──────────────────────────────────────────────────┐
│                                                  │
│                                                  │
│                                                  │
└──────────────────────────────────────────────────┘
```

Do I write people off whom I don't like even though they are my responsibility?

```
┌──────────────────────────────────────────────────┐
│                                                  │
│                                                  │
│                                                  │
└──────────────────────────────────────────────────┘
```

Do I try to be fair?

```
┌──────────────────────────────────────────────────┐
│                                                  │
│                                                  │
│                                                  │
└──────────────────────────────────────────────────┘
```

I hope that answering those questions was not too painful an exercise for you. But do you see the point? With the best will in the world we are not always as genuine as managers as we would like to be and this will lead to negative attitudes not positive ones.

Before we leave this section it's worth underlining the point made in passing above about non-verbal communication.

Imagine that someone is presenting a report to you about this month's sales figures and projections for the coming months. The figures might be good or bad, it doesn't matter. Think what non-verbal communication you would expect to see if the person were reporting to you in a positive rather than a negative way.

Jot down four things you would expect to see that non-verbally underline a positive approach.

_____   _____

_____   _____

You might have identified making good eye contact, sitting forward in your chair, open posture, enthusiastic tone of voice, neat appearance, smiling, supportive gestures. All of these would tend to support a positive attitude by the speaker.

Remember that, just as non-verbal communication can support a positive attitude, it can also 'leak' a negative one. If you think about it for a moment or watch for it in the workplace, you will be amazed at how often the motivation underlying what people say is given away by the failure of their non-verbal communication to support it. This is sometimes called 'leakage' where, for example, the speaker may be saying 'Thank you for a job well done', when in fact they are giving away the fact that they really don't think it was good at all, by the way they are standing, the rolling of their eyes or some other signal that shows they are not being genuine. This type of behaviour has no place in your positive attitude. Part of the art of being positive is to always try to be genuine and sincere and be careful that your non-verbal communication is giving the same message as you think you are expressing.

develop a positive self-image

When you look in a mirror, what do you see? Well, of course, you see yourself, but if you were to be asked to describe yourself, what would you say? The whole point about this is that if you do not respect and feel good and positive about yourself, how, as a manager, will you be able to respect and feel good about others? All too often managers are negative towards others because they feel frustrated or negative about themselves, and when others they manage are seen to do well, they cannot bring themselves to recognise it.

Let's note a few of the characteristics of people who have a healthy self-image, and are therefore far more able to adopt a positive attitude to the range of management skills they have. People with healthy self-image:

- ■ usually have strongly held views, and are willing to stick to them, but at the same time have the capacity to listen to and respect the views of others;
- ■ have a willingness to change, if they are shown to be wrong;
- ■ have confidence in their decisions and are not prone to feeling guilty or regretful about making them;
- ■ accept mistakes as part of a learning process without wallowing in them, and determine to find out what went wrong with a view to improvement;
- ■ feel equal to others, regardless of their skills or qualifications, and can accept their achievements with good grace;
- ■ are able to accept positive feedback;
- ■ think that other human beings are important and tend to look for the best in them;
- ■ are not shy about being emotional and don't see this as a weakness;
- ■ are not dominated by other people.

People with a healthy self-image make managers with a good, positive attitude! If you don't feel that you match up to all of those, don't worry, there is hope!

Try this exercise about your own self-esteem and then read the notes which follow for some advice about how to develop a healthy self-esteem.

Start by thinking of a time in your life when you felt really valued and your self-esteem was high as a result. Then think about a time when you felt utterly worthless, everything was going wrong and your self-esteem was at a low ebb. Let these form the two ends of a scale where 1 represents your lowest self-esteem and 10 represents the highest self-esteem you have ever felt.

Lowest self-esteem   **Highest self-esteem**

1   2   3   4   5   6   7   8   9   10

Now, think about how you are at work at the moment. Where, on your personal scale of self-esteem, do you currently fall?

Do the results indicate that you need to do some rebuilding work or are you all set to go for a positive attitude in your management?

If you do need to set about some rebuilding of your self-esteem, here are some practical tips to get you started:

■ Take a good, honest look at yourself and get back in touch with the real you, rather than the person you would like to be. This will give you some idea of how far you have to go and whether your expectations are realistic. Test out your answer to the question 'What's the matter with the way I am?'

■ Make an inventory of all your good attributes, first those that you like about yourself and then those that others like about you. Are you caring, attractive, intelligent, community minded ... whatever? Just make sure you focus on the positive aspects.

■ Consciously reject those aspects of yourself about which you are unhappy. Say to yourself that they are not important to you and that's all that matters. If there are problem areas which you can't ignore but can do something about, make a plan to get yourself to where you want to be.

■ Learn to control situations which you find difficult, or avoid them.

■ Only ever set realistic targets.

■ Learn always to say something good about yourself and your achievements.

Don't ignore your emotions. You need to learn to feel comfortable with yourself, the way you look and your skills inventory, and feeling comfortable has an emotional dimension.

being positive is not the same as not being negative

Before we leave this chapter it's worth noting that part of the art of being positive in your management skill is to recognise that being positive is not the same as simply not being negative. This is based on the principle that peace is not just the absence of war – it is something much more substantial than that. The fact is that being positive sometimes costs. This is particularly so in your role as manager when there will be times when you feel far from positive, but that feeling will be far from the way those you manage are feeling. You will owe it to them to suppress your own need in favour of theirs.

It would be all too easy to take the comfortable route out and adopt a neutral, non-commital position, but as a manager more is expected of you. Your positive attitude is crucial to those around you, your staff and your organisation, and all this is possible because you can choose to be positive even if you don't particularly feel like it:

■ You can choose to say positive things.

■ You can choose to give positive feedback.

■ You can elect to give a positive lead.
■ You can choose to act in positive ways.

summary

In this chapter we have looked at the art of being positive – some of the practical issues involved. Specifically, we:

■ reviewed some of the management skills to which you need to apply a positive attitude;
■ defined success and failure and noted that different people see them in different ways;
■ considered the importance of being able to receive positive feedback;
■ surveyed some of the ways of giving positive feedback;
■ thought about the importance of being genuine, including reinforcing sincerity with non-verbal communication;
■ noted how important a positive self-image is and considered ways to develop higher self-esteem;
■ noted briefly that being positive is a dynamic thing and not just the absence of being negative.

positive about performance

All modern organisations, whether they be in the public or private sector, are concerned with performance, both of the organisation itself and of the individuals that comprise it. There are a number of reasons for this, which include such factors as:

- performance can be measured;
- performance can be used to benchmark quality and success;
- performance can be used to compare organisations;
- performance can be used to develop targets.

One of the key areas in which your positive orientation as a manager will manifest itself is in the area of performance. As a manager you will need to be positive about poor performance as well as about good. Of course, in order to be positive about performance you need to develop the ability to identify exactly what constitutes good performance in your area of business, and, very importantly, be able to describe it as accurately and meaningfully as possible. This means that you need to be able to identify, and react to, good and poor performance both in yourself and in those who work for you. As a skill this will be useful to you in selection, appraisal and development of your staff. In this chapter, you will have the opportunity to:

- ■ identify the reasons why managing performance needs a positive approach;
- ■ explore positive approaches to failure to reach performance standards;
- ■ consider ways of positively managing disappointment;
- ■ experiment with positive and negative performance statements, or constructs;
- ■ develop constructs that describe the performance required in your own organisation;
- ■ consider ways of accurately describing performance.

identify the reasons why managing performance needs a positive approach

Let's start work on this section with a reflective exercise.

Identify all the people or groups (effectively stakeholders) who have an interest in and/or power over *your* performance as an individual manager within your organisation. The list below starts with a couple of suggestions as to who might have an interest in your performance as a manager. You might call them 'stakeholders in your performance'. Add to the list as many other stakeholders in your performance as you can identify. Then, and this is the reflective part, consider how a positive approach to your performance might affect that person or group. Try also to think what it would be like if you had a negative approach to your performance. An example is given to get you started.

Stakeholders in my performance	Effect of my positive approach to performance	Effect of my negative approach to performance
Customers	■ Customer satisfaction ■ Increased sales ■ Value added to the organisation	■ Loss of customer satisfaction ■ Potential failure to meet targets
Line managers	■ Confidence in my ability to be stretched ■ Able to delegate work to me ■ Happy to let me make decisions ■ Performance-related pay rise	■ Focus on me distracts from focus on organisational targets ■ Loss of confidence in my management ability ■ Performance-related pay reduction
Employees		
Senior managers		
Colleagues		

You will, hopefully, have been able to identify a number of 'stakeholders in your performance', and the effects that a positive or negative attitude on your part to performance might have on them. As a manager you will, in one way or another, be responsible for delivering performance not only of yourself but also others. The way you go about this will be crucial if you are to get the best out of them. In the reflective exercise above, you have already identified the importance of a positive orientation to your own performance. There are other ways in which managing performance needs a positive approach and they relate strongly to the way in which you manage the performance of others.

explore positive approaches to failure to reach performance standards

Let's face it, most of us do not willingly choose conflict as a way of going about our professional lives; many of us find it easier to be economical with the truth in order to have an easy life. If someone is under-performing, why go to the hassle of making an issue of it? Annual performance reviews, appraisals, performance development reviews or whatever they happen to be called in your organisation are a key area where you have an opportunity to demonstrate your positive approach to management even where you are addressing a failure to perform on the part of someone else. The way we handle failure will often be a good barometer of our skill as managers. Why is it important to positively manage a failure to perform? Some reasons that spring to mind include:

■ the needs of the organisation are not met by people who under-perform;

■ the needs of the customers or people who receive the service provided are not met by under-performance;

■ the individual who is under-performing cannot hope to change or improve unless he or she is given feedback about the areas in which there is a need for development (see Chapter 3);

■ your own management ability is called into question if you cannot positively handle under-performance.

Can you think of why, in your experience, positively managing under-performance is important?

Let's now consider some strategies for positively dealing with someone who is under-performing. As a way in to this, read the following case study and think about how you might deal with the situation. There are some questions to help stimulate your thinking.

case study 4.1
the skilled but temperamental team member

Kumari is a skilled member of your team. Your team's role is to produce marketing materials for clients. Kumari, along with the other three members of the team always gives 100 per cent in effort. She is rarely late for work and when she is it is because the trains have been delayed. She is both creatively and technically skilled and often does work of a quality that attracts praise from clients and others within the organisation. It would be difficult to run the team without her. Over the three years you have worked with her, however, Kumari has consistently shown a tendency to react to difficult situations with an emotional outburst that leads to her venting anger and frustration on you and anyone near her. This is a problem for others in the team who don't like it, and while she has never said anything directly to a client, Kumari will frequently say disparaging things about customers to the team. Your strategy up to now has been to ignore the behaviour, since after a period of sulking, Kumari usually comes round and carries on as if nothing has happened. As you now confront Kumari with your concerns in her annual performance appraisal, she does the very thing you wish to speak to her about and becomes angry and dismissive.

What are her strengths? Try to express these in performance terms.

What are her weaknesses? Try to express these in terms or why they may imact on other areas of performance.

What is the best way of dealing with Kumari in the appraisal interview?

What kind of development plan might be appropriate for Kumari?

case study 4.1 feedback notes
The skilled but temperamental team member

Actually dealing with Kumari in the interview in a positive way presents a difficulty because by the very way she reacts to these situations she is unlikely to be very responsive. A great deal of skill on your part will be needed if you are to get through to her. One thing that is certain is that you will need to strike the right balance. What it is you are trying to balance can be neatly illustrated in the diagram below.

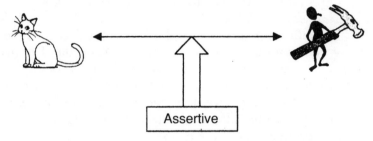

When we know that we will be confronting someone with diffi-cult behaviour it is all too easy either to pussy-foot at one end of the scale and not really address the issue, or to use a sledge-hammer to metaphorically batter them with. Pussy-footing may even allow the person to dominate the situation; sledge-hammering them may take away all their self-esteem and offer them no way out. What we need to try to do is be assertive, that is to make certain they know what behaviour it is that needs to be changed, but to end up with a plan that allows them both to maintain their self-esteem and also to have some-thing to work on. So how do you get Kumari to accept that her behaviour is having the effect that you say it is?

The key answer to this lies in the evidence, and the way you present it. The picture on the right is included to help you remember this point because it is vital. As human beings we are all

different, and one effect of this difference is that we all see the world differently. Now for practical purposes there are limits on the different ways people see things, but as a manager striving to be positive you need to recognise that not everyone will see the world in the same way as you do, and right and wrong are not always as clear cut as we would like them to be. In the Kumari case study, your first task is to establish whether she sees the situation in more or less the same way as you. A practical way of doing this is to follow some systematic steps:

1. Present the evidence for why you are saying what you are saying. This means that you need to be quite specific, and at this stage don't attempt to put an interpretation on it. So you might say 'Yesterday I noticed that you slammed the receiver back on the phone.'
2. Find out what the behaviour means. Instead of immediately making a value judgement, ask 'Why did you do that? What effect do you think that has on me and other members of the team?'
3. Secure agreement that the behaviour is not acceptable. If it is a problem for you only, don't try to pretend that it is a problem for others. Even worse, don't try to wriggle out of your responsibility by saying that you are only mentioning it because you have been told to do so. This sounds like you have no ownership of the issue at all, and you will probably make the situation worse not better.

Having worked through steps 1–3, you will need to make a plan with Kumari. Actually, to get the focus right Kumari will need to make a plan with your assistance. It is important that she has ownership of any development objectives that are set. Taking account of all that we have said so far, those objectives will need to be carefully constructed. A useful mnemonic to help you construct quality objectives is that they should be SMART:

Specific – focused on tightly defined areas of performance behaviour.
Measurable – it must be possible to know when the objective has been achieved.
Achievable – it must be within the capability of the person.
Relevant – the objective must address the problem in hand.
Time framed – a time should be set for review.

positively managing disappointment

For many managers, particularly those who care about the welfare and development of their staff, managing failure and disappointment is one of the hardest things to do. For most of us it's not only easier but also more pleasant to share good news with people than to confront them with their poor performance. To make matters worse, if you are the type of person who dislikes confrontation, then it will be doubly hard, since the natural reaction on the part of the person challenged is often to become angry, go into denial, seek to blame others or even accept it with a surly disbelief.

At the very centre of dealing with failure and disappointment, however, lies a core of opportunity to be positive and practise a positive attitude towards the way you manage. Let's look at some of those opportunities.

For you. You will be operating at one of the most challenging levels of your management ability. You will need to be:

■ sensitive to the needs of the person you are dealing with;
■ skilled in supportively confronting under-performance;
■ skilled in managing disappointment positively;

■ skilled in correctly analysing the problem so that you are focusing on the person's performance, not their personality;

■ positive about your own self-esteem so that you are able to be properly assertive and not aggressive or dismissive towards the individual.

For the person whose performance is poor or disappointing. They will be operating in a situation of maximum vulnerability and will need to:

■ move from a position of blame, denial or resignation to one of acceptance of the situation;

■ be able to understand, analyse and reflect on their poor performance and sign up to a way forward;

■ keep their self-esteem intact;

■ resist the natural inclination to deal with the situation by fighting back, blaming, denying, or becoming angry, all of which are likely to make the situation worse.

The following case study illustrates some of the issues about managing disappointment and failure that we have raised above. Read it through, think about how you might deal with the situation as a manager with a positive orientation and then try to answer some of the questions posed.

---

case study 4.2
the promotion candidate who hit a glass ceiling

Alex has been with her organisation for over 20 years. While her progress in terms of promotion has not been spectacular, she has gained a reputation for being highly competent and regularly performs the role that is required of the promotion grade she seeks, though she has not yet been formally promoted. Alex has passed the national exams that are required for the promotion, but her own large organisation requires her to pass a selection assessment centre to be promoted to the next grade. Despite meticulous preparation for the selection centres she has now failed on two occasions to be selected for promotion. Needless to say this has had a severe affect on Alex's self-confidence. She can quite clearly see where she wants to be but seems not to be able quite to make it.

Alex has come to you as a manager whom she recognises to be very positive in your management orientation.

> As a positive manager how would you approach Alex's problem?

> What advice, if any, would you give her?

case study 4.2 feedback notes
The promotion candidate who hit a glass ceiling

A priority with Alex would be to try to make sure that her self-esteem is not irreparably dented. She will need to be supported. She is a solid, long-serving member of staff with good performance appraisals and you will not want to lose her either by her resigning or by her losing her motivation to do well in the organisation. In short, you will not want her to lose *her* positive attitude towards self-development.

There will be a number of important issues to deal with as well as key questions that will need to be asked. All of this will need to be done in a supportive way. It is quite likely that as a person with so much experience Alex will not actually need you to give advice at all, rather she will need you to facilitate her thinking. Questions you may need to ask include:

■ How confident does she feel when she goes through the selection process?

■ Why does *she* believe that she is suited for promotion?

■ Is there any evidence that she is being discriminated against because she is a woman?

■ What does she believe is stopping her getting to where she wants to go?

■ Has she got the appropriate skills and experience profile to have a real chance of success?

■ If her experience or skill is lacking in some way, what would be the best way of her getting it?

■ Does she need to transfer to a different part of the organisation to get the breadth of experience that she needs?

■ Is further training needed?

Whatever the answers to these may be, there will be a positive or a negative orientation to the solution. It would be all too easy just to take the situation at face value and suggest that perhaps Alex hasn't got what it takes or even to try and persuade her that she should be content. But that would be to take a negative view of the situation. A positive orientation would be to assist Alex with her analysis of the problem. Find out, with her, the areas of weakness that she is experiencing and help her to develop a strategy to deal with them and turn them into strengths.

positive performance constructs

The subtitle for this section may seem a bit of a mouthful, but really it just means that performance nearly always has a positive and negative dimension to it. The term that is often used to describe these dimensions of performance is 'construct'.

If you glance back to the objectives at the beginning of this chapter you will notice that performance needs to be identified, defined in terms relevant to the area in which you are a manager and then described accurately. We will now consider some statements about performance, challenge you to apply these to your area of business, and then think about how performance can be described in positive terms.

experiment with positive and negative performance statements, or constructs

It is very likely that *communication* will feature as a common key area of performance for most people, so we will use that as an example. In the following table a number of positive statements about the way people communicate are made. Try to think of the negative dimension to each of the positive constructs and write this in.

Positive dimension	Negative dimension
Communicates ideas with clarity	
Uses jargon-free language	
Is sensitive to the effect of words on other people	
Communicates confidently	
Uses appropriate tone of voice	
Uses appropriate volume of voice	
Listens	
Effectively uses non-verbal communication	

So what has such a set of constructs got to do with a positive orientation to management?

Firstly, it is only really possible to be positive about performance if you, and the people you are managing, know what is expected of them. Written constructs help, in the areas of skill that are required of your people, to make sure that this is the case. Think back to what we said in this chapter about people seeing the world differently; one distinct advantage of written constructs about performance is that they help to secure agreement about what constitutes positive and negative performance.

Secondly, they can be used as indicators of areas for development. Take the constructs on communication above. A person may, for example, show a very positive performance in terms of their use of jargon-free language but may need to work on the area of their non-verbal communication. This may form a useful area for discussion in a performance appraisal.

Other typical areas of performance measurement might include:

■ decision-making;
■ leadership;
■ strategic/tactical thinking;
■ time management;
■ professionalism;
■ professional knowledge.

Each of the areas will have, as with the communication example above, sets of positive and negative constructs, to meet the performance needs of the organisation.

As a follow up to this it is suggested that you identify what areas of performance are required within your own management context. Then think about your response to these challenging questions:

■ Are the performance areas adequately defined by positive and negative constructs? Does more work need to be done to refine them?

■ When you are evaluating a person's or team's performance, are you doing so against the benchmark of known and published performance standards or against some arbitrary measure?

consider ways of accurately describing performance

To conclude this chapter about being positively oriented in your management of performance we will consider the important issue of recording performance observations. Very often the constructs that we have thought about above will be subject to some kind of scale that just needs a tick or a number to identify where on the dimension the performance sits. But selection, appraisal, references or whatever nearly always require some form of written assessment of the performance. Read through the extract from a written assessment taken from an annual appraisal of Mitul, a young man who works for an advertising agency.

Overall performance

Mitul has performed well this year as far as it goes. It has hardly ever been necessary to talk to him about meeting his performance targets and in the circumstances he has done surprisingly well. He is a popular member of his team and puts a lot of energy into activities outside of work. He runs a local football team and also arranges a number of social functions. There is nothing to suggest that he will not improve even more next year.

On the face of it Mitul's report is reasonable. But look more closely and find the following examples of negative reporting:

1. Statements that make a qualification: 'as far as it goes'; 'in the circumstances'. These are actually calculated to leave doubt in the reader's mind. What are these circumstances? What are the limits on his performance?
2. Comments that say one thing but mean another: 'Hardly ever been necessary to talk to him about meeting his performance targets' really seems to mean 'I have had to talk to him about his targets'; 'Surprisingly well' suggests that Mitul was not expected to perform well. The reader is left wondering why it was a surprise.
3. Why is there all the emphasis on what Mitul does outside his work activities? His prowess as a football coach has little relevance to how he performs at work.
4. Are the 'circumstances' a veiled indication of racial stereotyping on the part of the writer?

In reality the report lacks meaning and is helpful neither to the organisation nor to Mitul. Of course the passage itself is something of a caricature, but I hope you see the point that this is an example of negative performance description masquerading as positive.

There are some simple rules to follow to ensure that when you write about someone's performance it will be positive and helpful to all concerned:

■ Say what you mean, don't lace it with hidden coded messages.
■ Base your statements strictly on the agreed performance standards set for the individual.
■ Always take the trouble to give specific, actual examples of the point you are making and confine these to

performance at work, not what the person does in their own time.

■ Be scrupulous about challenging and eliminating any racial or gender stereotyping.

■ Be honest about where the person's performance lies on any given dimension.

■ Recognise that personality is almost never a relevant factor in performance.

summary

In this chapter we have looked at the importance of a positive attitude and orientation in the management of performance. This has included:

■ reflecting on why managing performance needs a positive approach both for yourself and for those who are stakeholders in it;

■ exploring positive ways of dealing with team members who are under-performing;

■ recognising the importance of striking an assertive balance between pussy-footing and sledge-hammering when dealing with under-performance;

■ considering the effect that differing ways of seeing the world may affect feedback about performance;

■ exploring the issues arising out of positively managing disappointment;

■ developing constructs for communication skills;

■ identifying some potential pitfalls in describing performance.

positive attitude in context

So far we have defined positive attitude, looked at some of the scientific principles underlying it, and thought about the art of being positive. This was followed by a chapter about performance. Now you are invited to start putting some of what you have been thinking about into context.

As you read through each case study, put yourself in the role of the overall manager of the person concerned. Try to answer the questions which follow and make notes of your answer. To give you an idea of how to approach it, you might like to glance at the feedback to one of the case studies; all the feedback notes follow after case study 5. You are not expected to write so much! Just jot down some notes.

---

case study 5.1
the nursery manager with no objectives

Emily is the manager of a children's day care nursery. She has been in the same post for a number of years and has become very friendly with a few members of her small staff. Your role as manager of a group of day care nurseries is to oversee the nursery managers and give them guidance, support and be responsible for them. You have noticed that on recent occasions when you have visited Emily's nursery, the place seems to be in chaos. Religious and secular festivals in the calendar which should be celebrated by the children seem to be missed, and on talking to the staff, you find that they don't appear to know what they should be doing. You speak to Emily and find that she has a negative attitude towards planning both long term and day to day; she tells you that she has been doing the job for years and sees little point in planning as she knows what to do anyway and so do her staff.

What particular management skill is Emily lacking?

How would you describe her attitude?

What would you say was Emily's main problem in this case? Suggest a solution.

How would you go about giving her feedback about her performance in a positive way?

case study 5.2
the banking supervisor who got the job done

Ferdinand is a supervisor in a large clearing bank. Having done the job for a number of years, he has noticed that times are changing, but he is not altogether happy with the way things are going. In days gone by, Ferdinand was judged by the efficiency with which all the business of the day was cleared, and whether the books tallied at the first or second attempt. This meant that the staff could get away on time and he was quite popular because the people who worked for him were rarely late home from work.

Recently, however, you have become concerned about Ferdinand because he seems to be quite unhappy most of the time. Whenever he speaks to you he tells you that he cannot understand what was wrong with clearing the day's business by hand and using calculators. He seems concerned that the technology he is now required to supervise will go wrong, even though it rarely does. You have tried to encourage him to take more interest in those who work for him, but he says that making the books balance is how he sees his role. You don't naturally like Ferdinand because he seems so negative about change and, apart from working for the same bank, you, his manager, have very little in common with him. You decide it is time to talk to Ferdinand about his attitude.

What management skills do you think Ferdinand needs to address? Refer to Figure 3.1 if you want a reminder to get you started.

Taking the skill you think he is in most urgent need of developing, devise a strategy that you could discuss with him as a possible way forward. Make a note of the key points of this strategy.

From what you know about the science and art of having a positive attitude, what dangers are there about Ferdinand's attitude that could affect the people who work for him?

In trying to give Ferdinand feedback in a positive way, what danger are *you* in?

case study 5.3
the personnel officer who couldn't accept feedback

Georgina is a personnel officer in your organisation and you are a colleague of hers of equal rank and status. Harry, a member of staff, approaches you and asks for a personal and private chat. Harry tells you that he has recently had his annual appraisal which was conducted by Georgina. Harry is quite upset because this year he was hoping for a good report from Georgina, as he was planning to apply to start training for promotion in the company.

He went into the appraisal with Georgina with a glowing report from his supervisor as this year he contributed greatly to the efficiency of his team's work, making membranes for medical face masks. He discovered that the problem of picking up more than one membrane at a time could be solved by using a vacuum tube adjusted precisely to the weight of each membrane. His team were delighted, his supervisor was delighted, but the personnel officer, Georgina, was completely underwhelmed by his achievement.

Harry is thoroughly fed up with the whole situation. When you ask him what he wants of you, Harry says that he would like you to have a word with Georgina. You agree. On speaking to Georgina about Harry's case she tells you that it's not anything to do with you and that she is quite sufficiently well qualified as a personnel officer to know what she is doing.

From what you now know about positive attitude, comment on:

Georgina's likely self-image.

Her attitude towards relationships with staff.

Her apparent inability to give positive feedback. Try to think of reasons why this should be so.

---

case study 5.4
the quality control inspector whose job it was always to find fault

Ian is a quality control inspector at your firm, which makes high-precision screw fittings for military aircraft. His main role is to act as quality controller for the dimensions of the fittings and this involves a complex series of measurements. Essentially, he is looking to find fault with either the dimensions of the screws or the process by which they were made. He takes his work very seriously and is determined that no wrongly dimensioned screw fitting will ever pass by him unnoticed. This type of positive attitude towards the quality control of the product is exactly what your company wants; the contract you have with the MoD depends on the exceptionally high quality of your product. Indirectly, lives and millions of people rest on the dimensions of the screw fittings.

The problem with Ian in the work setting, however, is that his ability to find fault extends not just to the screw fittings but to nearly all other aspects of his working life. Whatever it is, Ian can be relied upon to find fault with it, whether it be the canteen facilities, the toilets, the management, company policy, new entrants to the firm, people who are about to retire … whatever and whomever, Ian will find fault and criticise, mostly unfairly. His attitude is getting to the other staff and is undermining their morale, particularly as most people accept that Ian is actually very good at his job. He cannot see what he is doing and, as his manager, you have been asked to speak to Ian with a view to getting to the bottom of why he has such a negative attitude towards everything in the company.

As Ian's manager, make an assessment of his attitude. Where would you start?

What issues will you cover when you speak to him?

What strategies might you help Ian consider for his self-development?

Comment on the effect of a negative attitude in this sort of setting.

case study 5.5
the trainer who needed to learn that building people up works better than putting people down

Joanna is a trainer who works in a public sector government department. She has several years' experience and tends to favour the didactic, trainer-centred approach over the facilitative, student-centred one. Her normal job is to train new entrants in policy, procedures and the law relating to the business of the department. She feels very comfortable doing this because she knows more about the topic than the people she is training, and her teaching method makes her feel secure because there is little danger of new entrants being difficult or challenging. Joanna does this aspect of her job very well.

In a recent case of sexual harassment, which involved a member of the department, the tribunal noted the very poor arrangements for training the department staff in equal opportunities. You have decided that all staff need some training in equal opportunities in the workplace and several weeks ago tasked Joanna with the project. The first two-day course ran last week and was a complete disaster. Members of staff came to you and said that Joanna had accused them of being racist and sexist, and lectured them about the wrongs of prejudice and discrimination. Everything they said was challenged as being politically incorrect. They say that if nothing is done, they will go to the staff association and get a recommendation that no more staff attend the course.

Using your judgement in this situation, identify what is going wrong with the way Joanna is approaching this training.

What responsibility might you have for letting the situation get to where it is?

How can you apply a positive attitude to the situation which has arisen with Joanna?

feedback notes

These notes are intended as a guide only. Of course, there is no single correct answer to any of the situations; there are too many variables. You do, however, have sufficient information to be able to apply the basic ideas about positive attitude in management. So here are some suggestions as to the sort of responses you might have made in each case.

case study 5.1 feedback notes
The nursery manager with no objectives

What particular management skill is Emily lacking?
Clearly, Emily appears to lack skill in planning; the care and education of children obviously requires a high degree of planning and organisation to make it effective. It could also be that Emily has no idea of time management, and that is the reason why things are not getting done.

How would you describe her attitude?
Her attitude overall is clearly in need of some adjustment as things are not going well. It appears that there are three main worrying aspects about the attitudes she seems to display. The first is that she has an overall negative attitude in her responsibility towards running the nursery and is giving it very little direction. The situation where her staff do not know what they should be doing is having a negative effect on all of them. It would be interesting to know what effect the situation is having on the children.

The second is that alarm bells should be ringing about her friendliness with a few members of staff. This is a classic symptom of a negative attitude towards the need to be fair to all the staff. Leading on from this is the third point about fairness. What is her attitude towards equal opportunities? If there are children from minority ethnic or religious groups, Emily has a responsibility to cater for the multicultural aspect of childcare. Her attitude towards equal opportunities may well be negative and this is something which needs urgent attention.

What would you say was Emily's main problem in this case?
Suggest a solution.
As we have noted above, there are a number of problems with the way Emily is running the nursery, if you could say she is running it at all. Overall she appears to have a negative attitude towards her responsibility to manage and give direction. The solution may be to meet her to discuss the issues that concern you and make a plan with her for the situation to improve.

How would you go about giving her feedback about her performance in a positive way?
Your meeting with Emily is clearly not going to be easy. She has worked in the post for a number of years and her attitudes may well be entrenched and difficult to change. Since there are several problems, it might not be wise to tackle them all at once but deal with them in smaller chunks. Start by appreciating the things she is doing well but don't give the impression that you are building her up just to knock her down.

Assuming that you decide to start with the lack of direction and apparent lack of concern for multiculturalism, a positive way of handling this would be to describe to her very specifically and without exaggerating how you observe the nursery is working. Seek Emily's assessment of the situation before offering your own interpretation. Be firm that you want to see change but also be practical and develop a solution with her so that she has ownership of it. Some practical suggestions might include a regular staff meeting with an agenda and minutes taken, a plan to celebrate the next religious festival by involving all the staff in coming up with ideas, drawing up a weekly schedule of activity for the children, and so on. When these areas are working better, you could move on to other matters such as her potential exclusion of some members of staff by her friendliness with just a few.

case study 5.2 feedback notes
The banking supervisor who got the job done

What management skills do you think Ferdinand needs to address? Refer to Figure 3.1 if you want a reminder to get you started.
Ferdinand seems to have developed a negative attitude in a number of areas. He clearly cannot manage change and innovation very well, and seems to be less interested in the people who work for him than the processes he still tries to cling to. The key to his current attitude seems to be that he needs to be positive towards the management of change. He needs to adapt to new technologies and the practices they inevitably give rise to, and find other ways of feeling valued by his staff.

Taking the skill you think he is in most urgent need of developing, devise a strategy that you could discuss with him as a possible way forward. Make a note of the key points of this strategy.
Ferdinand needs to be able to cope with and manage change – this in itself is an indicator of a positive attitude. He needs to be able to identify why he feels change to be threatening. His concern that technology will go wrong is quite likely a smokescreen he is using to justify his position. In reality, he probably knows that he is not really being fair.

In commenting on the management of change in Chapter 1, we noted that one way of handling change, particularly technological innovation, is to have confidence in your ability to handle new things. If he can use a calculator, he would have had to learn to do so. If he was successful at that, why need there be a problem now? A positive way for him to approach this whole issue would be to identify what he finds difficult, and in the process sort out *training* needs from those which will be solved by him being more flexible in his attitude.

From what you know about the science and art of having a positive attitude, what dangers are there about Ferdinand's attitude that could affect the people who work for him?
We have already discussed that behaviour breeds behaviour and attitude affects behaviour. The situation with Ferdinand must not be allowed to continue because his negative attitude will inevitably rub off on those who work under him. If he has a negative attitude towards change, how can his staff be expected to be positive? They have no role model.

In trying to give Ferdinand feedback in a positive way, what danger are you in?
In giving Ferdinand feedback you will have to be on your guard that you do not treat him unfairly, or exaggerate the problem unnecessarily. The fact that you do not particularly like him could easily get in the way of your giving him feedback in a positive way.

case study 5.3 feedback notes
The personnel officer who couldn't accept feedback

From what you now know about positive attitude, comment on Georgina's likely self-image.
It is quite likely that, even though Georgina has reached a significant management position, she has low self-esteem. The indicators are there to see. She does not appear able to accept Harry's achievement. She is also unwilling to see that there might be a problem when you confront her, and hides behind her qualifications to do the job as if they make her immune from any criticism.

Her attitude towards relationships with staff.
She is clearly not comfortable with her relationships with staff. This negative attitude is obviously getting in the way of her work since her role includes the development and welfare of people and she cannot do this effectively unless she is more positive about her relationships with them, and more generous in her acceptance of their achievements.

Her apparent inability to give positive feedback. Try to think of reasons why this should be so.
There are a number of possible explanations why she is unable to give positive feedback to Harry. One could be simply that her own low self-esteem is getting in the way of her being able to see the good in others. Another is that she may receive very little reward herself and this is preventing her from giving it. It may be that her definition of success is widely different from Harry's and that she doesn't value a practical achievement as much as a paper qualification. All of these things, however, either singly or taken together, will tend to inhibit her ability to approach this aspect of her work with a positive attitude. If you want to review the advice about how to develop self-esteem positively, then look back at pages 48–51 in Chapter 3.

case study 5.4 feedback notes
The quality control inspector whose job it was always to find fault

As Ian's manager, make an assessment of his attitude. Where would you start?
Ian's case is not straightforward in that he quite clearly exhibits attitudes towards his work which are in fact very positive and precisely what the company wants. The problem is that, although he is very positive about quality control, he is negative to the extent that he is undermining the morale of the other

staff with whom he comes into contact. Ian is exhibiting a judg-mental attitude which will get in the way of his being positive.

What issues will you cover when you speak to him?
Clearly, there is a real sense in which Ian is an asset to the company and future contracts will depend on a consistently high level of quality control. To give him feedback in a positive way you will need to stress his value and worth to the company. Having said that, you cannot avoid the fact that you will have to confront him with the way in which he is under-mining morale. The way to do this, however, is to focus on the behaviour and not to label him as some kind of subversive. Try to find the reason for his negative attitude. Is there a problem which you could help solve? Is he happy? Does he need a change?

What strategies might you help Ian consider for his self-development?
There are a number of strategies which could be tried to assist Ian to make an attitude shift. An obvious one is to involve him in a positive way in some of the aspects about which he is complaining. If there is a canteen committee, could he be involved with it? Would new entrants to the firm benefit from a spell under Ian's wing to learn the importance of quality control? Does he need to be given more responsibility?

Comment on the effect of a negative attitude in this sort of setting.
One of the problems which will arise if such a negative attitude is allowed to take root is that eventually something will suffer. We have already seen the morale of the staff suffer, and it is quite likely that before long the quality or quantity of the production will suffer also.

case study 5.5 feedback notes
The trainer who needed to learn that building people up works better than putting people down

Using your judgement in this situation, identify what is wrong with the way Joanna is approaching this training.
On the face of it, Joanna's approach to this problem is all wrong. Her tendency to didactic training could well be getting in the way of her ability to deal with a sensitive subject properly. She is approaching the topic in a very negative way, and experience has shown that with this type of training, taking an accusing stance rarely works very well. Learners, many of whom are actually well intentioned, just build up feelings of resentment.

Racism and sexism are particularly sensitive areas which take people out of their comfort zone, often to face issues that they would prefer not to address. Joanna may feel that if she maintains a didactic style she will avoid getting into the murky waters of how people feel about these issues. The problem with this is that she mistakenly believes that by merely pointing out the faults in people they will respond with learning. Unfortunately, life is not that simple; learners respond better to being built up rather than being put down.

What responsibility might you have for letting the situation get to where it is?
As Joanna's manager you may bear some responsibility for what is going on. How much could you reasonably have expected to know about her training method and ability? Prior to the event, did you discuss the course objectives and the methods she would use?

How can you apply a positive attitude to the situation which has arisen with Joanna?
A number of issues in this case study need the application of a positive attitude to repair and progress from a difficult set of

circumstances. Joanna needs to have a more positive attitude towards training methods and content which may not be her style or with which she may not be familiar. It may be that you, as Joanna's manager, need to take a more positively proactive approach to her development and also a more active role in what she is doing. As regards the staff she has upset, you will need to be very positive in the way you handle their problem if they are not to be completely alienated from the pursuit of equal opportunities.

summary

Using some cases drawn from the experience of the real world, we have seen how some of the aspects of positive attitude can be applied.

■ Case study 1 revolved around positive attitude towards planning and direction.

■ Case study 2 centred on the need for a positive attitude to the management of change.

■ Case study 3 focused on self-esteem and being able to receive feedback.

■ Case study 4 looked at the way a negative attitude can undermine morale and affect others around, even though the job is being done.

■ Case study 5 looked at the need for a positive attitude towards learners, and how a positive attitude is needed to move out of the areas in which we feel comfortable.

the benefits of a positive attitude

So far in this book we have identified positive attitude, considered the science and art of adopting a positive attitude, focused on performance and, in the last chapter, considered some of the implications of a positive attitude in practice. In this and the next chapter we will start to draw the threads together, first by identifying the value-added aspects of a positive attitude. You will be challenged to consider the lessons of the previous chapter and now move forward to apply the learning to your own work setting or other context in which you are reading this book.

After you have worked through this chapter I anticipate that you will:

■ Be able to identify the benefits of a positive attitude in terms of the benefits to
   – yourself;
   – people whom you manage;
   – people who manage you;
     your clients, customers and the commentators on what you do.

■ Be able to summarise the benefits of a positive attitude
  in terms of
  – feeling good about yourself;
  – the effect of positive attitude on a team;
  – the response of clients, customers and commenta-
    tors;
  – the way in which positive attitude can unlock doors
    to:
    (a) new targets;
    (b) greater efficiency;
    (c) better sales;
    (d) better service;
    (e) higher output;
    (f) better quality output;
    (g) better motivated and more satisfied staff.

Let's consider the benefits of a positive attitude as a series of
concentric circles. If you throw a pebble into a pond, even a
small pebble, you should notice that there is a considerable
impact where it lands. Then the ripples start to move outwards
in ever-widening circles and you find that the initial impact
of the pebble has had an effect quite disproportionate to
its size.

The same effect is to be seen when managers have a positive
attitude to all the aspects of their management skill. The effect
of that positive attitude will have benefit not only for the individual manager concerned but also to an ever-increasing circle
of influence.

Figure 6.1 illustrates what we have been saying. Use it as an
exercise to identify as many benefits of a positive attitude
relating to the appropriate circle as you can. I have suggested
one benefit in each category to get you started, but you should
be able to think of many more.

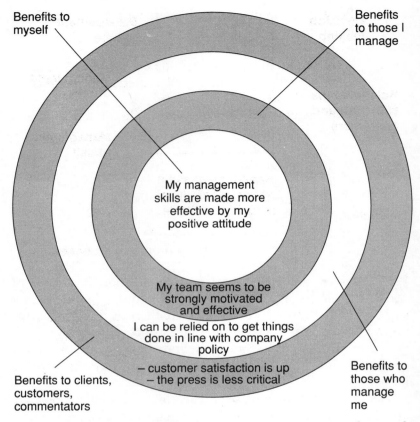

Figure 6.1 *Benefits arising from a positive managerial attitude*

benefits to yourself
you will be more effective as a manager

If we can permit a little self-indulgence for a moment, it has to be said that the benefits to you of adopting a positive attitude are considerable. In Chapter 3 we identified a number of management skills, as reproduced again on p. 89, which you as a manager need, all of which benefit from the application of a positive attitude.

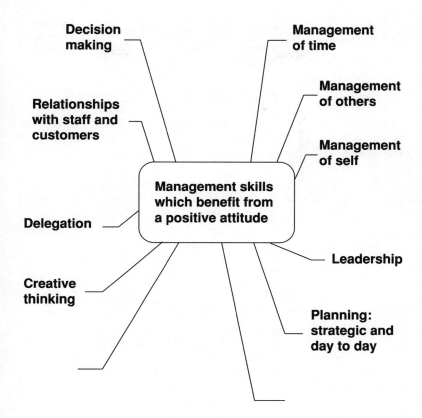

Figure 6.2 *Aspects of management skill improved by a positive attitude*

Let's consider just two of these skills in a structured way. Remember that these are my ideas and by no means all may be relevant to you. You will have other issues. Two blank grids follow so that you can use the same structure to carry on with the other skills if you choose.

	How I could apply a positive attitude to this	Benefits to me
Management of time	■ Set targets each day ■ Learn computer diary! ■ Recognise the need ■ Don't say yes automatically ■ Have fewer meetings ■ Make meetings fruitful ■ People before tasks	■ Things get done ■ Priorities are met ■ I can relax more ■ Less stress ■ More organised ■ Less worry

	How I could apply a positive attitude to this	Benefits to me
Decision making	■ Know where I am going ■ Listen more ■ Ask more ■ Know more background ■ Consider options ■ Consider consequences ■ Who needs to know? ■ How to communicate it? ■ Stick by decision	■ Become decisive ■ Appear decisive ■ Gain respect for fairness ■ Do my job better ■ Develop management skill ■ Time saved in long term ■ Efficient use of time

	How I could apply a positive attitude to this	Benefits to me
(skill)		

	How I could apply a positive attitude to this	Benefits to me
(skill)		

you will feel good about yourself

There is another benefit of a positive attitude which will accrue to you personally. You will feel better about things. Being positive means knowing where you are going at work, even in life generally, and doing the things you need to do to get there most easily. By and large, people with a strong positive attitude will also have an appropriately high level of self-esteem and self-respect. This leads to confidence in yourself and your management skill and this in turn facilitates your ability to approach problems with a positive attitude – it becomes a cycle of reinforcement.

your career prospects will be enhanced

You may not be particularly career minded in the sense that you want advancement. You may be happy at the level you have reached and just want to continue doing a good, effective job. Either way, a positive attitude will help you.

Performance-related pay, annual career appraisal and so on, are a reality for most of us and a negative, couldn't-care-less attitude is the last thing we need to be confronted with when others are appraising us. On the other side of the coin, if that negative attitude is the way we approach work, how can we expect more of those whom we manage and have to report on?

benefits to those whom you manage

What benefits did you identify in the concentric circle exercise on pages 87–88? Here are a few more you might like to think about.

■ They will be working for a better manager. Let's face it, if you were to draw up an inventory of the attributes of the person you would most like to manage *you*, they would have a strong thread of positive attitude through them. We have already mentioned genuineness, respect and other qualities, which roll together to make a good manager. A benefit to your staff is simply that they will be working for a good manager rather than a bad one.

■ They will work more effectively together. It is my experience of working in a variety of team and group settings that the way the team works together has such a close connection to the manager's attitude that you would not be able to slide a piece of paper into the gap! If your team is doing well, think about how much that might be related to your attitude.

■ They will be better motivated. In Chapter 2 we established that motivation is the satisfaction of needs, drives and incentives. Your positive attitude will influence *your* motivation and, in turn, will influence *theirs*. You will be creating the climate they need to thrive and develop. For example, if members of your team have a need to be creative, they will be better motivated if *you* are positive about giving them opportunities to develop this creativity.

■ They will have a good role model on which to base their own attitude to work. At the very beginning of the book the point was made that many of our attitudes are *learned*. One way in which this happens is that we select people on whom we consciously or unconsciously model our behaviour. Therefore, a benefit to your staff of your positive attitude towards management is that they will have a good model from which to learn. For example, if your attitude towards deadlines or quality of customer care is positive, then theirs has a far better chance of being so too. If you are not positive in such areas, what incentive do they have?

benefits to those who manage you

While we are not making too much of this point, it is worth noting that your positive attitude will also have benefits for those who manage you. Did you identify any in the exercise on pages 87–88? Here are some possible ideas for you to consider:

■ Your managers will be able to rely on you to get things done in line with company/organisational policy.

■ The quality and efficiency of the service or output for which they are ultimately responsible will be enhanced.

■ There will be fewer problems to solve, allowing more time for proactive and constructive development rather than reactive damage limitation.

■ The organisational aims are more likely to be met, especially if, through the positive attitude of yourself and others, a climate of positive attitude is developed within the organisation. This in turn can lead to raised morale of the workforce.

■ Management becomes *quality management* rather than mere supervision.

benefits to clients, customers and commentators

Who do we mean? Well, ultimately we are nearly all engaged in activity which provides a product or service to people either directly or indirectly. Think for a moment about who your clients are and who your customers are. There is little doubt that the words mean different things to different people, but in this context clients are taken to be people with whom you probably have some kind of contractual agreement. Clients may be within your organisation or outside it. Customers are those who, in the broadest sense, are on the receiving end of what you do. So they may be receiving the service you provide or the product you make, or they may be the people you sell to.

Commentators include all those who have an influence on the way people think about the organisation you are in. They may be journalists, contributors to professional journals, reviewers, ombudsmen, governing bodies, in fact any individual or group who has an influence over the way what you do is perceived.

Before moving on to a final exercise in this chapter, let's glance at a few of the benefits of a positive attitude to these groups, starting with clients and customers.

clients and customers

New targets will be set and met. A positive attitude towards getting things done in the best possible way, whether it's production targets, response times, waiting times, shorter lists or faster delivery, will be better for the customer or client. The speed at which paperwork is dealt with is an obvious example. A positive attitude towards the quality and speed of response to correspondence can have great benefit for the way a customer sees an organisation:

■ more efficiency;
■ better service;
■ better quality output;
■ greater confidence.

The trend over recent years has been to move away from monopolies towards competition. In addition, the concept of

Citizens' Charters has increased the pressure to provide a higher level of service. Whatever you might think of these trends, the reality is that whether you like it or not the public is becoming more discriminating when it comes to being on the receiving end of service. A traditional, if slightly mythical, British willingness to stand in a queue is being replaced by a demand that the telephone is answered by the third ring, letters are answered in three days, and waiting to be seen should be shortened to a level that is acceptable to the customers not the service provider.

In what ways can a positive attitude both by you and your staff improve the service you provide?

---

commentators

It has become obvious that no institution is sacred and no institution is immune from being scrutinised from all sorts of angles about the way it operates. Now, while you may have mixed views about such developments, there is little doubt that great damage can be done to the reputation of an organisation if negative attitudes prevail within it. A selection of examples of the sorts of issue which might be picked up on include:

- fairness in the way staff and customers are treated;
- integrity, particularly of those who make policy and are then seen to break it;
- lack of concern for the environment in production methods;
- lack of integrity in the application of the law;
- dishonest selling practices;
- taking advantage of vulnerable groups in society.

The list could go on almost indefinitely. But the point to be made is that such issues will only be addressed if individuals within organisations bring a positive attitude to bear, so that integrity, honesty and so on become important within an organisation and a positive climate is built up. The organisation, and individuals within it, will be less vulnerable to negative comment by commentators who have an interest in it.

future action challenge

Being able to see the benefits of a positive attitude in the short, medium and long term can be a huge boost to your motivation to improve your own attitude and learn more about the areas of your own management which need addressing. Let having a vision of the benefits of your positive attitude be your incentive.

Think about your own situation at work from the four perspectives we have used in this chapter. You will find four circles below. In each case think carefully about the *extent* to which the benefits of a positive attitude are being reaped, and shade the circle with a pencil to represent that amount. Now consider the blank area of the circle and its size. What do you need to do to enable you to fill the circle as much as possible?

summary

We have started to draw some of the threads together by surveying the benefits of a positive attitude in your management.

■ The benefits were seen as a series of concentric circles, radiating from the benefits to yourself to the benefits to your clients and customers.

1. To what extent are you aready reaping the benefits of a positive attitude?

   For yourself?

   What do you need to do to enable you to shade the circle fully?

2. To what extent are you aready reaping the benefits of a positive attitude?

   For those you manage?

   What do you need to do to enable you to shade the circle fully?

3. To what extent are you aready reaping the benefits of a positive attitude?

   For those who manage you?

   What do you need to do to enable you to shade the circle fully?

4. To what extent are you aready reaping the benefits of a positive attitude?

   For your clients and customers?

   What do you need to do to enable you to shade the circle fully?

■ We noted that three of the benefits to you as a manager are effectiveness in your management skill, higher self-esteem and enhanced career prospects.

■ There are also benefits to those whom you manage, and we noted among these motivation, effective teamwork and a good role model to follow.

■ There are also benefits for those who manage you, in that you will be an effective member of the organisation because your positive attitude will lead to quality management.

■ Finally, we identified that your clients and customers benefit in a variety of ways and, in today's climate of competition and emphasis on quality of service, you cannot ignore the importance of positive attitude.

■ The chapter concluded with a challenge to you to identify the areas in which there are more benefits to be reaped and what you need to do to obtain them.

five golden rules for having a positive attitude

In this chapter we will draw together all the threads of what we have been saying so far and consolidate them into five golden rules for a positive attitude. After you have worked your way through this chapter I expect that you will:

- have identified the five golden rules for having a positive attitude;
- have evaluated the extent to which you already follow the five golden rules;
- be in a position to plan your future action in relation to your own positive attitude.

So what are the five golden rules for a positive attitude?

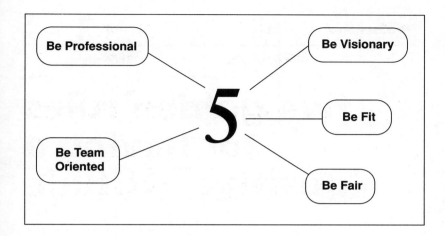

be professional

The word 'professional' has taken on a much wider meaning in our language than just referring to those who work in the traditional professions, lawyers, doctors and so on. When we say professional we generally mean to describe the way someone goes about their work. Therefore, the first golden rule for a positive attitude in management is to be professional. What does the word mean to you? Try the next exercise.

Imagine for a moment that an English-speaking alien has landed from another planet, and is trying to find out as much as it can about your work and management practices. You happen to drop the word 'professional' into the conversation. 'What's professional?', it asks in a metallic voice. What would you tell it?

Note down some of the words which spring to mind. The alien requests that you also tell it the word which means the opposite to the concept which you are using to describe professional. Two examples are given to get you started.

'Professional'	Is	Is not
	Integrity	Dishonesty
	Quality	Second rate

How did you get on? Were you able to find words to describe how you understand the concept of being professional? Review your list for a moment and consider the positive and negative descriptions you have given. How do they relate to having a positive attitude? More importantly, how do they relate to *your* positive attitude?

Look at the characteristics of being professional you have identified and write them down in the three groups below.

My professional strengths	My professional characteristics which are adequate	My professional weaknesses – which need improving

I hope that by now you have agreed that there is a strong link between a positive attitude in management and professionalism. Also, by now, you should have realised why the boxes are different sizes, but just in case you weren't getting the message, I didn't give you enough space to wallow in too much negative thinking about yourself, but gave you plenty of space for your positive attributes. Do you see how the negative characteristics are just things which will get in the way of your having a positive attitude in all your management skills? In the boxes above you will have grouped the characteristics in three categories.

your professional strengths

Provided you answered honestly, celebrate these:

- Use them.
- Role model them.
- Let them underpin your positive attitude.

your professional characteristics which are adequate

In terms of self-development, realistic targets is always the name of the game. Attempting to change too much too quickly generally means that we end up changing nothing much at all! So, if you have many items in the third box, you might need to put what is merely adequate on to the back burner for a while. If your third box is empty, which of your adequate professional characteristics are most in need of your attention? Remember that all the time the aim is to be professional through being positive.

your professional weaknesses

A feature of almost all people who purport to be professional is that they are usually unwilling to accommodate weaknesses in that professionalism. There will be a positive attitude towards change and self-development which will tend to make the person want to be as effective as they can. If you have honestly identified a weakness in the characteristics of your own professionalism then do something about it:

- Decide to take action; without actually making a decision to do something you probably never will.
- Plan a way of addressing the weakness and turning it into a strength. Do you need help or can you work out a plan for yourself?
- Do it. Put your plan into action and remove a barrier to your positive attitude.
- Remember to keep your objectives 'SMART'.

be visionary

A positive attitude in management will often, if not always, be accompanied by what we might call *vision*. This means having a clear view of where you are going. If you have a positive attitude about yourself, you will almost certainly know where you are going. But, as a manager, you will also know where your team is going and where your organisation is headed. If you know where you are going, those you are managing have a far better chance of knowing where they are going. If you do not know where you are heading, how can they be expected to know?

be positive about where you are going

Start by asking yourself a few simple questions and writing the answers in the spaces below.

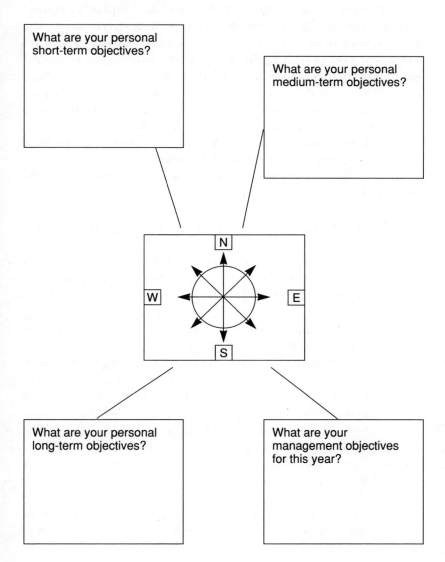

What are your personal short-term objectives?

What are your personal medium-term objectives?

N

W

E

S

What are your personal long-term objectives?

What are your management objectives for this year?

How easy or hard did you find it to answer the questions? If you found it hard, the chances are that you are not at all positive about where you are going. Now throughout this book we have not used the word positive to mean *certain*. But in this context there is a sense in which people who display a positive attitude through being visionary do know where they are going and are usually certain (in the other sense of positive) about it.

Having said that, it really is surprising how many of us are not at all positive about where we are going, even in the short term. You know the feeling; the time for your annual appraisal comes round and you wax eloquent about the achievements of the past year. Then comes the question 'And where do you expect to be going, taking your team (or whatever) in the next year?', and you are literally lost for words.

To be positive is to be visionary. Here are some tips about being visionary:

- Invest some time in thinking about where you are going. It's amazing how little we actually stop and think. I once knew a very senior adviser in my own organisation who made it his purpose at the start of every day to sit at his desk and *think*. For him it was as essential a task as reading the papers, journals, going to morning prayers, or whatever. It was part of his management skill ... and it showed.
- Consider it your management responsibility to know not only where your team is going, but also the ways in which you can best communicate that. There is little point in having a crystal clear view of where you and your team are heading if you have no hope of communicating it.
- Give those you manage the inspiration they need to want to go in the same direction. As we will see below, positive teams pull together.
- Make sure you are in a position to demonstrate to those who manage you that you know the aims,

mission or goals of your organisation and are taking active steps to meet them.

be fit

The third golden rule for a positive attitude is to make sure that you are fit. This means giving yourself the best possible chance of adopting a positive attitude by feeling as physically and mentally good as you can.

Try answering 'Yes' or 'No' to the following questions; tick the appropriate box.

Yes No

☐ ☐ Do you often feel unusually tired?

☐ ☐ Do you often feel that you can't be bothered to get on with the things you know you must?

☐ ☐ Do you believe you get enough sleep?

☐ ☐ Do you feel you can take a day off work occasionally without everything going wrong at the office?

☐ ☐ Do you sometimes feel it's all getting on top of you?

☐ ☐ Are you sometimes irritable with your colleagues or those who work for you?

☐ ☐ Are you very overweight?

☐ ☐ Assuming there is no medical reason why you cannot exercise, are you generally unfit?

☐ ☐ Do you often skip lunch?

☐ ☐ Do you often miss breakfast?

If you answered 'Yes' to any of the questions above, there is probably something you can do to remove a potential obstacle to your own positive attitude. Think about some of them.

tiredness

Have you ever seen children who are overtired? They become irritable, uncooperative, deny there is a problem; in fact they exhibit all the sorts of negative traits we witness in colleagues daily. This not only confined to children, adults can suffer from it too! Thinking we can get by with little sleep is often a misconception. We all have a limit to how long we can go on without the quality of what we do falling off rapidly. Be aware that you too have a limit, and that your positive attitude will suffer or disappear altogether if you are tired.

bad eating habits

Nearly all the medical advice you will come across about your health and well-being will include advice about diet. Eat sensibly and try not to skip meals too often. Most people agree that there is a good chance your performance will be impaired if you miss breakfast. Do you really need always to skip lunch only to have a huge meal in the evening? Such habits just might indicate that you could do more to take control and look after yourself better. Having a positive attitude towards your management will be much harder if you do not have a positive attitude to a healthy diet.

fitness

You cannot fail to have noticed the explosion of physical activity which has taken place over the past few years. Jogging, cycling, swimming, weight training and aerobics in all its forms have all become popular with many people. Why do they do it? Well, one answer must be that people are beginning to value personal fitness much more than used to be the case. Many people who exercise do so not only for health and fitness and to help control their weight, but also because it makes them feel *good*. It's easier to be positive if you feel good than if you don't. It's as simple as that!

stress

Most of what we have discussed above relates to physical aspects of your well-being. Stress, however, is a phenomenon that touches us all, is underrated by some and will definitely have an adverse affect on your positive attitude if you allow it to. There are many complete books on stress and its management that will help you if it is an issue for you. To round-off our thinking about fitness as a golden rule for a positive attitude it is worth making a few comments about our psychological fitness as well as physical.

The problem with stress is that it can be a good thing – such as a motivator of people, as well as a bad, even dangerous thing that can result in severe adverse physical reactions.

Look at the following list of potential *emotional* reactions to stress in your life. Tick the ones that you feel might have an adverse affect on your ability to be positive.

You are under pressure to do something you feel you can't cope with.	
You find it difficult to talk about how you feel.	
You feel frustration and aggression about little things as well as big.	
You fear failure.	
You fear social embarrassment.	
You find it hard to enjoy things you normally would – food, entertainment and so on.	
You feel you can't take a day off work.	
You feel mentally drained.	
You feel you will burst if you take on something else.	

How many did you tick? Even one tick may mean that there are stresses in your life that may get in the way of your positive attitude. So what can you do about it? Ideally talk to someone who you know can help without judging you. Or you could start with getting hold of a book to help you think through the issues. Whatever you do, don't see drinking, smoking or over-eating as ways out. They are impostors.

Other strategies include:

■ Keep a stress diary. This will help you identify patterns and unmask underlying causes.
■ Adopt a rational problem-solving approach to your issues.
■ Talk to someone – don't feel you are above professional counselling.
■ Confront your stresses head-on and make them your slaves not masters.
■ Learn to say no.

future action challenge

Think about your own fitness and the way it relates to your positive attitude. Then make some resolutions if you think they are necessary.

In relation to my sleeping patterns I intend to:

In relation to my eating habits I intend to:

In relation to my fitness I intend to:

In relation to my stress levels I intend to:

be fair

So far almost nothing has been said about equal opportunities. Yet one of the golden rules for a positive attitude is to be fair; that is what equal opportunities is all about.

- ■ Unfair selection
- ■ Discrimination
- ■ Harassment
- ■ Prejudice

are all the result of a negative attitude towards fairness. As a manager you have a legal and moral duty to be fair to those who work for you. This is not just the duty of the equal opportunities officer or personnel officer, it is *your* duty to know about, practise and role model fairness.

There are myths and complicated legislation in relation to equal opportunities which can make the whole subject seem obscure and sometimes even irritating. But don't worry! Being fair in the workplace is mostly common sense and there are a few principles for being fair which will fit almost any situation. Just remember that any unfairness on your part is a huge barrier to your own positive attitude in management. Colleagues, customers or clients may forgive you for mistakes, delays, even incompetence, but you will rarely be forgiven for being unfair. People expect, and have a right, to be treated fairly.

Here are six suggestions for checking out your own attitude towards fairness and assessing whether it is positive or negative. We might think of them as bricks in a wall which forms a barrier against discrimination and prejudice. How well built is your wall?

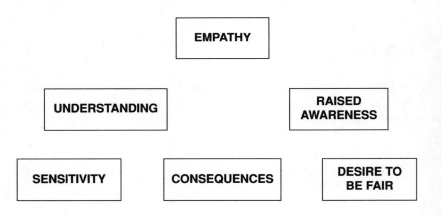

empathy

Empathy is not the same as sympathy. It is about trying to reach an understanding of how the other person might be feeling, without necessarily feeling the same way as they do (which is more to do with sympathy).

Take time occasionally to think about how it might feel to be on the receiving end of unfairness. If you are a member of a minority group in this country, you will sadly not have too much difficulty in doing this. If you are a member of a majority group, however, it is quite likely that you take an awful lot for granted, and you will often need to pull yourself up and think about the potential unfairness of a given situation.

understanding

Much unfairness is caused not so much by evil intent as lack of understanding of the mechanisms involved. Nearly always attitude will be involved, and very often the attitude will be negative rather than positive. Think about:

■ The ways in which your own attitudes might amount to prejudice.
■ The ways in which your attitudes can affect your behaviour (see Chapter 2).
■ The types of behaviour which will lead to unfairness.
■ The consequences of your attitudes (see below).

raised awareness

An implicit theme of this whole book has been the need to be in control of yourself and your development and to make changes where necessary. Raised awareness of issues about fairness will help you to do this. Do people really have to 'take you as they find you' or are there areas in which you could, if you chose, make changes? Make an effort to be more aware of:

■ Your own prejudices – where they come from.
■ Your use of language – is it always appropriate?
■ What you know of other people and their needs. Do you know the best way to help a deaf person to lip read what you are saying?
■ What you know of other cultures. Do you just see them as a threat or do you celebrate diversity?

In all these you will be positive about broadening the horizons of your awareness.

sensitivity

Through understanding, empathy and raised awareness you cannot help but become more sensitive. This does not mean soft (although there's nothing particularly wrong about that) but it does mean that you will not 'put your foot in it' nearly so often!

Being sensitive to:

■ thoughts;
■ needs;
■ feelings;
■ opinions

in other people, particularly those you come into contact with as a manager, those who work for you, clients, colleagues and customers, is an essential thread to weave into being positive.

Are you always as sensitive to the needs and feelings of others as you could be?

consequences

Almost everything we do, every decision we take, everything we say will have one or more consequence. An essential component of being positive about being fair is to make a conscious effort to identify the consequences of an action, decision or conversation, and decide whether it will have any unfair effect.

Here are some sample questions to illustrate this:

■ Do I really need to make this joke? Will it hurt the person who is the subject of it?
■ Is this decision likely to have an equal effect on everybody it refers to?
■ What are the consequences of my staying silent? Will I be seen to be concurring with bad behaviour?

■ Will this action be fair as well as appearing to be fair?
■ What are the consequences of this action for ... a particular minority group? Will its effect seem to be racist, sexist or discriminatory towards the disabled?

Such careful attention to the consequences of what you do and say will pay big dividends for your positive attitude.

desire to be fair

The last brick in our wall against unfairness is simply a *desire* to be fair. It's a lot easier to be positive about being fair if that is what you really want. Just paying lip service to fairness will very quickly be spotted.

Keep the notion of fairness and promoting equality of opportunity at the top of your personal agenda and you will not go far wrong.

be team oriented

Unless you have some specialist function in which you work entirely alone, it is almost inevitable that you will be either responsible for or work in a team. In a moment we will take a look at the characteristics of an effective team and you will see how a positive attitude is a golden thread which is woven through almost everything that relates to team effectiveness. Remember that your attitude will affect not only you but the team also, and team members will influence each other.

While the following list is neither exhaustive nor in any particular order, it contains the main characteristics that you would expect to be evident in an effective, smoothly operating workplace team:

■ Team members are all involved and interested in the aims and goals which the team is working towards.

■ The goal towards which the team is working is agreed to and signed up to by each member of the team.

■ Team members listen to each other.

■ Creative thinking is encouraged.

■ Disagreement is faced head on rather than turned into a hidden agenda. It is then resolved or accepted with good grace.

■ Most of the important strategic and tactical decisions are arrived at by consensus and not imposed by an 'authority' figure within the team.

■ Criticism is always constructive and focuses on issues and not individuals.

■ Team members are clear about their roles and responsibilities within the team.

■ Leadership of the team may shift according to the expertise and knowledge of people rather than always being given by the person who is nominally in charge.

■ Evaluation of what is going on is a welcome and accepted part of the process the team goes through to achieve its objectives.

You will probably be able to think of some other characteristics of an effective team that you are in or know about, but for the time being let's work with the list above. We said that there is a golden thread of positive attitude present in a team which is working well. In the next exercise some of the key words which represent this golden thread have been isolated and made into a table.

Have in mind a team you have contact with, preferably one you are responsible for, but failing that, one you are in or one you know about. For each of the 'threads', think carefully about whether that particular characteristic of team effectiveness is working or not working, and attempt to rate it on a scale of 1 to 5 where 1 represents not working at all, for example no one in the team ever listens to any other, and 5 represents the characteristics always being present in the team and always working well. Circle the number on each scale which you think fits best.

Positive characteristics in teams	My rating of a team (I lead, am in or know of)				
	Not working			**Working well**	
Involvement	1	2	3	4	5
Interest	1	2	3	4	5
Listening	1	2	3	4	5
Creative thinking	1	2	3	4	5
Resolution of disagreement	1	2	3	4	5
Consensus	1	2	3	4	5
Constructive criticism	1	2	3	4	5
Clear roles	1	2	3	4	5
Clear responsibilities	1	2	3	4	5
Leadership shift	1	2	3	4	5
Evaluation	1	2	3	4	5

Now add up the total of the positive attitude rating you have made. [   ]

A score of 11 means a team which is full of negative attitude towards almost every aspect of its work, whereas a score of 55 means that your team is probably not only composed of human beings! You must make the judgement about what the score means for yourself. Having said that, you may well have revealed an overall picture of the positive attitude in your team and also identified some individual characteristics that need working on.

future action challenge

Which areas of team orientation do you need to work on as an individual?

What will you actually do to effect change?

summary

In this chapter we identified five golden rules for a positive attitude: be professional, be visionary, be fit, be fair and be team oriented.

- Being professional is far easier if it is grounded in a positive attitude. You were invited to consider your professional strengths and weaknesses, and apply a positive attitude to developing areas of weakness.
- Being visionary is all about knowing where you are going and being able to communicate that vision to others in a way which will inspire. We noted that setting aside time just to think, represents a positive use of your time and will help you to sort out the way forward.
- Being physically in good shape plays an important role in being able to adopt a positive attitude in management. We cannot all be Olympic standard in our sporting prowess, but there are few of us who cannot eat a healthier diet, take a bit more exercise and have an early night occasionally!

■ Being fair is an essential ingredient in your positive attitude because it affects almost all aspects of your decision making. People who work for you expect and have a right to be treated fairly.

■ The last of the five golden rules is to be team oriented. This means that your management should focus on the importance of the team and by encouraging and modelling positive attitude, the potential for team effectiveness will be greatly enhanced.

Visit Kogan Page on-line

Comprehensive information on
Kogan Page titles

Features include

- complete catalogue listings,
  including book reviews and
  descriptions

- on-line discounts on a variety
  of titles

- special monthly promotions

- information and discounts on
  NEW titles and BESTSELLING titles

- a secure shopping basket facility
  for on-line ordering

- infoZones, with links and
  information on specific areas of
  interest

PLUS everything you need to know
about KOGAN PAGE

http://www.kogan-page.co.uk